T0114718

His Glorious Angels

Calling in Angelic Intervention through
Prayers, Dreams, and Spoken Words

SHERYL A. GLASS

WESTBOW
PRESS®
A DIVISION OF THOMAS NELSON
& ZONDERVAN

WestBow Press books may be ordered through booksellers or by contacting:

WestBow Press
A Division of Thomas Nelson & Zondervan
1663 Liberty Drive
Bloomington, IN 47403
www.westbowpress.com
844-714-3454

Scripture taken from the King James Version of the Bible.

ISBN: 978-1-6642-4091-9 (sc)
ISBN: 978-1-6642-4090-2 (e)

Print information available on the last page.

WestBow Press rev. date: 7/26/2023

Contents

Acknowledgments

MY FIRST AND FOREMOST ACKNOWLEDGMENT GOES TO GOD. IT IS THROUGH HIM and His works that this book has been realized. It is for His glory that this book was developed and written. I'm hoping to discover more about Him on my journey.

I dedicate these writings to my dad. He has been a real motivation for sharing his personal experiences and information concerning angels. It is my hope that others are enlightened and know more about how angels operated in the Bible and our present daily lives.

To my decedent father, Arthur Morris Philpot, thank you for being the light in my world and a beacon of light for others. He talked about angels often to my daughter and me. I never thought about angels that often, until my father constantly made mention of their great aid. Dad's angelic experience will be written about in this book.

I am grateful to my mother, Lorene Philpot. You are a faithful steward toward your missions and goals. Your faithfulness to complete tough tasks is inspiring and your presence, comforting.

To my cousins Angela, Kimberly, and Zenobia, you are very special. Shout out to my aunt Annie Johnson for her contributions as well.

Special thanks to Mr. David Charles Turner. I thank you for being an instrument in building my faith in difficult times and introducing me to gospel music that I enjoy.

You're always available to help those that need guidance, thank you Theophilus S. Glass.

A warm-hearted thanks to Dr. Debbie Green and Candace Byrd. You have no idea how we appreciated your caring hand during family challenges; during the times we needed you to be there. You were right there at the right time.

Special thoughts to Aunt Winnie, Lisa, Bridgette Philpot, Mint, Marcy, and all the Philpot family for their warm embrace.

I cannot disregard my faithful neighbors Ujima Thomas, Anita, and Brandon Bundrage. Thank you Ujima, Brandon, and Anita for the support you have given to our family. It is appreciated more than you know.

I'm giving a special thanks to my daughter, Jenay Lyles. She helped me to edit this book. She gives her tireless dedication to helping others. Jenay provided inspiration, that created in me a desire to keep writing. She never wanted credit for assisting me.

To my son-in-law Jordan Lyles, you're always there to lend a helping hand. I want to simply say, thank you for your assistance.

To my son, Tobias D. Turner, thank you for the insight that you have given into my life. Your input is valued more than you know. God bless you Tobias as you move forward with your life goals.

I dedicate this book to my grandchildren also. My love and prayers are always there for you. I'm glad that you are in my life.

I would also like to give special thanks and acknowledgment to the late Joseph Meekins, who was an important individual in the life of the family. He loved helping people in the best ways that he could. He was always concerned about the suffering of others.

Thanks, Annette Valenza for your interest and caring concern for those you love. Ciara Turner and Stephanie Terry, you are loved. You are appreciated for keeping a loving heart and staying in touch with your loved ones. God bless you, as you accomplish your heartfelt goals and dreams.

Introduction

THE MAIN PURPOSE OF THIS BOOK IS TO BRING TOGETHER A BRIEF COMPILED outline of the works of His Glorious Angels. The writings include how angels direct us to the glory of God's miraculous hand, and how they operate in our daily lives. Angels are involved in the healings, deliverances, miracles, judgments, and redemptive works of Jehovah (God). Angels have operated in the lives of God's prophets and people throughout the Old and New Testaments. God's people received intervention from angels in many ways. He still uses angels in this present time.

Though the topic of angels is still considered mystical in some cultures, they are still very active in this present day. Some people may feel that considering the existence of angels is not important. However, the many miraculous interventions that angels perform for God give a valid reason for an interest in them. It is my hope that you can gain more of an understanding of angels and how they operate as you read this book.

I'm not conveying that I have expert knowledge concerning angels or angelic encounters. My experiences, I feel, have been several encounters involving angelic interventions and earth angels that will be shared here. Most of the information concerning angels is taken from the Christian faith, the Holy Bible. The scriptures used in these writings are from the Old and New Testaments. I started writing this book in 2018. I stopped writing and started back again in 2020. 2020 is the year that the pandemic began in the world. A time in the world when angels were needed and thought more of for protection.

When I first began writing about angels several years ago in 2018, it was not that difficult. The further I researched the topic, the realization dawned on me of the complexities of the subject. It was an experience of deep humility to realize that writing about this powerful subject would not be as easy as I thought. It was a feeling of awe before God as well. According to the New International Encyclopedia of Bible Characters (2001), there are approximately 292 references to angels in both the Old and New Testaments of the Bible. Within the Old Testament, there are 114 references to angels and 178 in the New Testament.

The journey to write about angels felt at times challenging. Often, in the past, I could write papers without struggling to write them about many different subjects. This book was a different situation. I'm thankful for the helpers that God sent my way. I could not progress without them.

When looking online for research concerning the evidence of angels, I found a book called Proof of Angels by Ptolemy Tompkins and Tyler Beddoes (2016). This book explains how it feels for most authors to write on the topic of angels which I understood to be factual. These authors mentioned that it has always been difficult to write about angels for various reasons. This explained to me why I faced the difficulties that I had. The difficulty came for me as well when discovering that this book would have to be much longer than I expected to write. For many years I have read the Bible and never noticed how much angelic activity was really in there. The many areas to cover regarding what angels did in the Bible, I felt had to be written about. It was an eye-opener for me to discover the revelation of how angels intervened in many areas of life in the Bible, which should not be overlooked. Learning more about angels is a very worthy subject to embrace.

❧ What Are Angels?

The word angel comes from the Greek word *angelos*, which means *messenger, or one who is sent*. Mal'akh is the general word for angel in modern Hebrew. They are spiritual supernatural beings created perfectly. The Holy Bible does not give us information about angelic genders. However, whenever an angel delivered messages to people, that specific angel appears as a human male. The human form is used to calm fears in order that the person may listen and talk to that angel without fear. This is said because when angels appear in their angelic form human beings usually are very afraid and in terror.

Angels are invisible and are not seen unless God wants them to be seen. Balaam the non-Israelite prophet in the Bible, could not see the angel standing in his way until the Lord opened his eyes to see the angel (Num. 22:31). The angels of God are invincible and have never been defeated on their missions for God. Some individuals can see angels. God is the one that opens their eyes to see angels.

Angels are Spiritual Beings

According to the Holy Bible, angels are immortal spiritual beings created by God to act as His servants and emissaries. The Bible acknowledges that God has an order of spiritual beings which are said to rank above human beings but under God. Angels are primarily intermediaries between God and human beings. They are said to know everything except what depends on human choice and God has not revealed. Angels are said to reside in the Kingdom of God, also serving as guardians and protectors. Those who have witnessed angels usually describe them as swift bright lights. Some describe them as human-like figures with wings.

Angels have also been known to take on human form in various situations. Over centuries, many religions, and cultures have depicted angels as symbols of healing, protection, guidance, virtue, and intercession. Because of this, it cannot be implied that God's angels only come to those within a specific religion or culture. Angels have also been known to make appearances through subconscious faculties, usually through dreams and visions.

The Existence of Angels

Angels existed before humans were created by God. Angels rejoiced with God when He created the earth. In the book of Job within the Old Testament in chapters one and two there is written the words or phrase sons of God. This phrase refers to angels. They are the sons of God. In Job 1:6 the verse talks about the sons of God, "Now there was a day when the sons of God came to present themselves before the LORD, and Satan came also among them." The sons of God which are supernatural heavenly beings, mentioned in Job 1:6 are angels.

In the book of Job, the sons of God are represented as appearing before the throne of Yahweh or Jehovah (God) in the heavens. They were ready to serve Him. In Job 2:1 it states, "Again there was a day when the sons of God came to present themselves before the Lord, and Satan came also among them to present himself before the Lord." Some theologians and ministers believe that these verses of scriptures that refer to the sons of God in Job 2:1 and Job 38:7 refer to the angels of God. Whereas there are certain scriptures in the New Testament that the words sons of God refer to those that are led by the Spirit of God. Romans 8:14-17, 1 John 3:1-2, Matthew 5:9, and Philippians 2:15 are scriptures referring to the sons of God as those in the body of Christ, God's children. There are other scriptures in the New Testament as well that reference the body of Christ being sons of God. In the Old Testament, the term sons of God in Genesis 6:1-3 may be a reference to the fallen angels.

Sons of the Mighty God

They shouted for joy at the creation of the earth. In the book of Psalms, the angels celebrate the glory of Yahweh (the Hebrew name for God). Angels are called the sons of the mighty in Psalm 89:6, "For who in the heaven can be compared unto the Lord? Who among the sons of the mighty can be likened unto the Lord?" They are also called morning stars in the Old Testament within the book of Job, chapter 38:7. Biblical scholars believe that morning stars in verse seven chapter 38 of the book of Job, are referencing to the angels. The phrases morning stars and sons of the mighty are examples of Hebrew parallelism. Hebrew parallelism is basically defined as using a variety of words to express the same thoughts (House to House Heart to Heart, 2016).

Yes, the angels witnessed God making the heavens and the earth. The heavenly host of God. It states in Job 38:4-7, "Where wast thou when I laid the foundations of the earth? declare if thou hast understanding. Who hath laid the measures thereof, if thou knowest?"

or who hath stretched the line upon it? Whereupon are the foundations thereof fastened? or who laid the cornerstone thereof; When the morning stars sang together, and all the sons of God shouted for joy?" Angels are intelligent non-human beings. According to these scriptures, we can conclude that the angels were God's original family from the beginning before human life.

The holy angels and the fallen angels both have free will. In the book of Isaiah 14: 13-14, Satan is having a dialogue concerning how he will lift himself above the Highest God in heaven. The scriptures state he wanted to be like God, because of his pride. He led a third of the angels in rebellion who were cast out of heaven. Those fallen angels chose to follow Lucifer. As human beings, we have the choice of free will also. This example shows us that the holy angels that stayed in heaven with God made the choice not to follow Lucifer.

Seeing Angels

ANGELS ARE NOT VISIBLE TO THE EYES OF HUMAN BEINGS, AS MENTIONED EARLIER. Angels are spirits according to the scriptures. Hebrew 1:7 states, "And of the angels he saith, Who maketh His angels' spirits, and His ministers a flame of fire." However, some individuals can see into the spirit realm and can see angels. Various occurrences involve people seeing them during biblical times and our present times.

God can open the physical or spiritual eyes of anyone He chooses; even animals sometimes can see angels. Elisha, the prophet in the Old Testament prayed for God to open a nonbeliever's spiritual eyes. Elisha wanted their eyes to be opened and can see in the spiritual realm. His prayers were answered (2 Kings 6:17).

An Animal Seeing an Angel

Here is a specific example of an animal seeing in the spirit realm, in the book of Numbers chapter 22 verses 21-27. God opens the eyes of a donkey that belonged to the prophet Balaam to see an angel. "And Balaam rose up in the morning, and saddled his ass, and went with the princes of Moab. And God's anger was kindled because he went: and the angel of the Lord stood in the way for an adversary against him. Now he was riding upon his ass, and his two servants were with him.

And the ass saw the angel of the Lord standing in the way, and his sword drawn in his hand: and the ass turned aside out of the way and went into the field: and Balaam smote the ass, to turn her into the way. But the angel of the Lord stood in a path of the vineyards, a wall being on this side, and a wall on that side. And when the ass saw the angel of the Lord, she thrust herself unto the wall, and crushed Balaam's foot against the wall: and he smote her again. And the angel of the Lord went further, and stood in a narrow, where was no way to turn either to the right hand or to the left. And when the ass saw the angel of the Lord, she fell down under Balaam: and Balaam's anger was kindled, and he smote the ass with a staff."

The Prophet Seeing the Angel

In Numbers 22: 31-33, God opened the spiritual eyes of the prophet Balaam and then he was able to see the angel too. "Then the Lord opened the eyes of Balaam, and he saw the angel of the Lord standing in the way, and his sword drawn in his hand: and he bowed down his head and fell flat on his face. And the angel of the Lord said unto him, wherefore hast thou smitten thine ass these three times? behold, I went out to withstand thee because thy way is perverse before me: And the ass saw me and turned from me these three times: unless she had turned from me, surely now also I had slain thee, and saved her alive."

Mary and Archangel Gabriel

In the Bible Mary, the mother of Jesus was afraid when she saw the angel, Gabriel. Luke 1: 28-31 reads the following, "And the angel came in unto her, and said, Hail, thou that art highly favored, the Lord is with thee: blessed art thou among women. And when she saw him, she was troubled at his saying, and cast in her mind what manner of salutation this should be. And the angel said unto her, Fear not, Mary: for thou hast found favor with God. And behold, thou shalt conceive in thy womb, and bring forth a son, and shalt call his name Jesus." When reading throughout the Holy Bible, there is always a common reaction of fear when angels are presented to people to bring messages and insight.

Thoughts of Angels

I can only imagine how Mary felt when she saw the archangel, Gabriel. The experience of even thinking about seeing an angel was frightening to me. I knew within myself that God was going to allow me to see an angel. He wanted to open my spiritual eyes. The thought of it continually came to my mind for months. The thoughts would come out of nowhere, that I would indeed see an angel. When these thoughts would come to my mind, I would pray to God for it not to happen out of fear. The simple idea of seeing an angel intimidated me. It was difficult to understand just why I would need to see one.

During the time when I was captivated by thoughts of probably seeing an angel. I was working at my home with severely handicapped children. Some of the children were sick and had to stay home and be seen around the clock if needed. A hospital bed was sent from medical supplies by the foster care company if it was necessary. I felt that God was pleased with the decision to take care of foster kids that did not have a home or parents.

My spouse was also in agreement about taking in foster children, to give them a stable loving home and family. Deciding to make the children a part of my family life and career was refreshing for me. I enjoyed working with the children. However, it was challenging when they would get sick or have difficult behavior issues.

We had special classes from the agency designed to attend on a consistent basis that gave us instructions and advice on how to best take care of the children. In those classes, we met other foster parents that enjoyed what they did. Most of them were very dedicated to the tasks of caring for the children. Some of the kids had difficult behaviors to manage as well. The training was mandatory to stay abreast of how to best meet the needs of these special kids.

I truly felt at that time in my life that God had directed me to this path of taking care of foster children. I was happy about trying to be the best parent that I could be. During this specific time in my life, two angelic miracles happened to me, while taking care of special needs children. Some of the children were medically fragile and in wheelchairs.

I was taking care of a young girl of about 14 that was bedridden most of her life. She also had a severe eating disorder and had to be fed a special liquid diet around the clock. The liquid had to be measured out precisely. Her social worker would come just about every other day and stay for a couple of hours. She was there to see how everything was going, and to obtain current paperwork that I had documented on her activities and medication intake.

The weight of the responsibility became a lot, and I was not getting enough rest or free time to refresh myself. The consequences were that I became very sick. I had no one to assist me with helping if I became sick. Everyone around me worked during the day or was involved in other activities outside the home. I was so sick that I could barely walk or drive down the street to the hospital.

When I finally got waited on the doctor told me that I had double pneumonia. He gave me some medicine and I went home. I turned on some gospel music on my favorite Direct TV music channel, took the medicine, and crashed into bed. I never thought of why I was sent home as sick as I was. I kept thinking repeatedly that I had no one to help me get certain activities done for the children or help me around the house during the daytime.

I saw an Angel Fly

Out of nowhere, here comes an angel, just when I was almost asleep. At first, I thought oh no it's time for me to die and leave the earth. He is coming to get me. I was kind of intimidated by his presence. However, I was very sick and because of that issue, I could do nothing but stay in bed and watch wherever the angel went.

I just watched the angel as he flew around my windows, which he did after being around my cable tv box where the gospel music was playing. He was the most beautiful being I have ever seen in my life. The bright, white-colored robe and white wings were the most glorious white that I had ever seen here on earth before. I do not feel the need to discuss the skin tone or hair color of this angel. He did have a human form with wings.

I thought that I was hallucinating or that the medicine was too strong when I first saw the angel. From previous experiences, I knew that antibiotics would not make me hallucinate. This was my third time getting pneumonia and I knew that the medications were not the reason why I was seeing the beautiful, winged celestial being (angel) in my bedroom. As I stated earlier, I was almost asleep before seeing the angel. When he got to my window it looked as if he had disappeared; after seeing him there I closed my eyes and went to sleep. I don't know what happened next that day.

When I awoke in the morning the next day, the double pneumonia was gone. I did not feel sick anymore. I felt normal and completely healed. Praise be to God, that cared to send me some help. God knows I had plenty of responsibility and was very sick with no one to help me get better. God (Jehovah) is so kind and merciful to humans that try their best to help others with kindness and care. I was able to start my day and take care of my children and special needs children. Honestly, I don't know why I was chosen to see an angel but I'm glad that God allowed one to come by to see about me.

Divine Intervention from Fire

The second angelic miracle I received while taking care of special needs foster children was being saved from a house fire. Remember, I shared earlier that some of the special children had difficult behavior problems. We had a teen of eighteen years old that burnt his aunt's trailer down to the ground and she no longer was able to take care of him. One day a friend of my mother asked him to wash dishes in a stern way that he did not like. The young man went to his bedroom angry without my knowledge.

Around the late evening, my thoughts were that I needed to anoint my bedroom. I did not know why these thoughts continued to be on my mind. Finally, I did get some olive oil and only anointed the walls in my bedroom. Afterward, I got in my bed and went to sleep. Then suddenly, I was awakened, I heard my mom's friend yell, "the boy has a huge fire going in his bedroom!" The young man had his bed on fire and the fire rapidly went to the curtains, on the floor and most of his room was burnt. The fire was almost all over his room and my room was right next to his bedroom.

I thank God for sending His angelic intervention to give me divine directions that night. The fire never touched my room. The fire did not come to the side of his room which was near my bedroom. Usually, my mom's friend is not over at our house that often. I asked the young man why he set the fire. He said nothing, however, my mom's friend replied that he got very upset when he was asked to wash dishes. He did not like the tone of voice used when he was being asked to do the chore.

❧ For His Glory

Angels receive their power from Jehovah (God), to help convey His messages, deliverances, and many other glorious works. Angels are not to be worshipped. Nehemiah 9:6 states, "Thou, even thou, art Lord alone; thou hast made heaven, the heaven of heavens, with all their host, the earth, and all things that are therein the seas, and all that is therein, and thou preservest them all, and the host of heaven worshippeth thee." The Lord made the heavens, the earth, and all heaven's angels. Angels can best be thought of as His agents on Earth.

God is the one that directs angels to do whatever He commands on earth and in the heavens. According to Luke 1:26, God sent the archangel Gabriel to the city of Galilee named Nazareth where Mary was located. "And in the sixth month, the angel Gabriel was sent from God unto a city of Galilee, named Nazareth." As we read here, it specifically lets us know that God sent the angel Gabriel.

The angels are specifically created for His Glory and to do His will. For instance, Colossians 1:16 states that God created the angels. "For by him were all things created, that are in heaven, and that are in earth, visible and invisible, whether they be thrones, or dominions, or principalities, or powers: all things were created by him, and for him." Angels are not like humans. The scriptures tell us that angels are created specifically to listen to and obey God.

Angels Commanded to Worship God

Psalm 103:20 says, "Bless the Lord, ye his angels, that excel in strength, that do his commandments, hearkening unto the voice of his word." Thus, we can conclude that angels serve special purposes for God. Just as God created humans for His glory, He also created angels for His glory. Hebrews 1:6, states God's purposes for the angels. "And again, when he bringeth in the first begotten into the world, he saith, and let all the angels of God worship him." We see here that angels are given special directives and permission to worship God and Jesus Christ, God's son.

Angels Causing Death to Herod

God has given us understanding in Isaiah 42:8 about how serious He is about His Glory. "I am the Lord: that is my name: and my glory will I not give to another, neither my praise to graven images." Here is another example of what an angel did to Herod when he did not give God the glory. "And upon a set day Herod, arrayed in royal apparel, sat upon his throne, and made an oration unto them. And the people gave a shout, saying, it is the voice of a god, and not of a man. And immediately the angel of the Lord smote him because he gave not God the glory: and he was eaten of worms, and gave up the ghost" (Acts 12:21-23). The angel of the Lord put Herod to his death.

Angels know that God must get His glory. They will direct you to give glory to God and not to worship them. Angels will direct the attention back to God. "For mine own sake, even for mine own sake, will I do it: for how should my name be polluted? and I will not give my glory unto another" (Isaiah 48:11). God admonished us to give Him the glory for everything; "Whether you eat or drink or whatsoever ye do, do it all for the glory of God" (1 Corinthians 10:31).

Why is it necessary to give God glory? One reason for this I feel is that God wants to be acknowledged as our source for all the good that He has given and done for us. He is the one that controls and sends angels to assist in times of extreme importance. He desires and deserves all glory because He is God.

Angels At Jesus' Resurrection

The angels were eyewitnesses to Christ's resurrection from the dead. During Jesus crucifixion the Bible says in the Gospel of Matthew chapter 27: 51- 54 that a violent earthquake occurred. Three days after the death of Jesus Christ Mary Magdalene and the other Mary went to the sepulcher (Matthew 28:1). There was another great earthquake because the angel of the Lord descended from heaven and came and rolled back the stone from the door of Jesus' tomb and sat upon it (Matthew 28:2).

The scriptures tell us that the angel's countenance on his face was like lightning, and raiment white as snow. "And the angel answered and said unto the women, Fear not ye:

for I know that ye seek Jesus, which was crucified. He is not here: for he is risen, as he said. Come, see the place where the Lord lay. And go quickly and tell his disciples that he is risen from the dead, and behold, he goeth before you into Galilee; there shall ye see him: lo, I have told you" (Matthew 28:3-7).

When the Lord Jesus Christ was in His resurrected body and about to ascend into Heaven, the Bible says the angels were not only in Heaven watching his ascension, but two angels were also on earth watching the event. As Jesus ascended into Heaven, the crowd was gazing into the sky. And those angels said to the crowd, "Men of Galilee, why do you stand looking into the sky? This Jesus, who has been taken up from you into heaven, will come in just the same way as you have watched Him go into heaven" (Acts 1:11).

❧ Calling in His Angels

We can conclude from the scriptures in the Bible, that if we as believers of His Word rely on the scriptures and speak them with conviction for specific needs, angelic help will occur on our behalf. Remember this, the Bible reveals the true power of spoken words. At certain times, we can wonder why certain events are happening in our lives that we do not understand or like. There are specific occasions in life in which looking back can provide some insight. For emphasis, look at how you spoke concerning that situation.

If you spoke negative words instead of God's Word, which are positive words, then you may have created resistance, which limits the intervention that the angelic hosts are able to provide. The book of James illuminates the powerful element of the tongue. "And the tongue is a fire, a world of iniquity so is the tongue among our members, that it defileth the whole body, and setteth on fire the course of nature; and it is set on fire of hell" (James 3:6).

Understanding the Power of Our Words

Truly understanding the power of words, confessions, and decrees is necessary. Take another look at how powerful words are and your intentions. James 3:6 said that the tongue can set a person's entire life on fire. The word of God also tells us that death and life are in the power of the tongue (Proverbs 18:21). This scripture tells that whatever you say can preserve your life or destroy your life. Spoken words are very powerful. God created the world and everything in it, with His Words in the book of Genesis.

The Fear of the Lord Brings Deliverance

Another important aspect to look at when considering angelic intervention is what the scripture Psalm 34:7 reads. It says that "The angel of the Lord encampeth round about them that fear Him, and delivereth them." Reflect on how God had placed a hedge of protection around Job in the Bible. The Bible states that Job feared God.

He was blameless and upright. God had a conversation with Satan about Job. Job 1:8 gives an example of having the fear of the Lord. "And the Lord said unto Satan, Hast thou considered my servant Job, that there is none like him in the earth, a perfect and an upright man, one that feareth God, and escheweth evil?" What does it mean to fear God? Reading the book of Job in the Holy Bible gives insight into how a person lives when they fear God.

Angelic Dreaming

Angelic help can come to us in many ways and forms. God can still speak to us through dreams as He did in biblical times. There are instances in the Holy Bible where angels have come into dreams to give guidance and insight into situations. Sometimes when prophets were spoken to by God in the Bible, they were spoken to in dreams. There are recorded events where angels have acted on behalf of mankind through dreams.

Your dreams do not have to include an angel to be considered prophetic or significant. For instance, in Genesis 37 Joseph had two dreams that he shared with his relatives. The two dreams did not mention an angel of the Lord; however, the dreams were very significant and prophetic. They foretold the future of Joseph and his family.

God can show urgent information through all kinds of channels, which may include dreams. Angels do send messages through dreams sometimes. If Jesus Christ, angels, or

God does appear to you in a dream, know that it is an important message that should be taken seriously. Angels may also communicate with us through repetitive thoughts that provide instructions or insight, deep feelings, and synchronistic signs. The prayers of faith bring God's assistance. He sends His angels to help us and to provide answers to prayers.

An angel came to Joseph in a dream and gave Joseph instructions. "But while he thought on these things, behold, the angel of the Lord appeared unto him in a dream, saying, Joseph, thou son of David, fear not to take unto thee Mary thy wife: for that which is conceived in her is of the Holy Ghost" (Matthew 1:20). The angel gives Joseph and Mary insight into what to name the baby and the great purposes of Jesus Christ to the world.

❧ The Messengers of God

In Acts 27:23-24, we witness in the Word of God how an angel spoke to Paul and told him things to come, "For there stood by me this night the angel of God, whose I am, and whom I serve, Saying, Fear not, Paul; thou must be brought before Caesar: and, lo, God hath given thee all them that sail with thee."

Angels Appearing to Mankind with Messages

Luke Chapter 1 provides details about how an angel of the Lord came to deliver a message to Zacharias about his wife Elizabeth. The scriptures state that Zacharias and Elizabeth both were righteous and walked blamelessly in the ordinances and commands before God. Luke 1:7 provides the details of their situation. "And they had no child because Elisabeth was barren, and they both were now well stricken in years." The angel of the Lord appeared to Zacharias, and he was afraid. The angel told him to fear not and that his prayers were heard. He was told that his wife would bear a son and his name would be John.

The angel identified himself as Gabriel which spoke to Zacharias. Gabriel gave Zacharias messages of insight concerning the will of God. Luke 1:14-17 states the following concerning the birth of his son. "And thou shalt have joy and gladness, and many shall rejoice at his birth. For he shall be great in the sight of the Lord and shall drink neither wine nor strong drink; and he shall be filled with the Holy Ghost, even from his mother's womb. And many of the children of Israel shall he turn to the Lord their God. And he shall go before him in the spirit and power of Elias, to turn the hearts of the fathers to the children, and the disobedient to the wisdom of the just; to make ready a people prepared for the Lord."

There are other angelic messages delivered to the people of God in the New and Old Testaments. Here in Genesis the 18th chapter, Abraham has 3 angels appearing unto him. These angels appear to Abraham in human form. Genesis 18:1-2 states, "And the Lord appeared unto him in the plains of Mamre: and he sat in the tent door in the heat of the day; And he lifted up his eyes and looked, and, lo, three men stood by him: and when he saw them, he ran to meet them from the tent door, and bowed himself toward the ground."

These 3 angels that came to Abraham gave him the message that he and his wife will have a son in due season. When the angels found out that Sarah laughed at the idea of having a child in her old age, the angel repeated the prophecy again in Genesis 18 verse 14. "Is anything too hard for the Lord? At the time appointed I will return unto thee, according to the time of life, and Sarah shall have a son." These 3 men were indeed angels of God. In verse 22 of Genesis 18, it says "And the men turned their faces from thence and went toward Sodom: but Abraham stood yet before the Lord."

These men were the same angels that went to destroy Sodom and Gomorrah. "And there came two angels to Sodom at even; and Lot sat in the gate of Sodom: and Lot seeing them rose up to meet them; and he bowed himself with his face toward the ground" (Genesis 19:1). In the 19th chapter of Genesis, the 1st verse, reads that the angels that Abraham had in his presence went to Sodom.

Samson's parents were greeted by an angel. The angel gave the woman a message that she would have a child (Judges 13:3). "The angel of the Lord appeared unto the woman and said unto her, behold now, thou art barren, and barest not: but thou shalt conceive, and bear a son." This angel predicted the birth of Samson. The angel also instructed her that she should not drink wine or any alcohol nor eat anything unclean while carrying the baby. "For, lo, thou shalt conceive, and bear a son; and no razor shall come on his head: for the child shall be a Nazarite unto God from the womb; and he shall begin to deliver Israel out of the hand of the Philistines" (Judges 13:5).

Angels and Elijah, the Prophet

Angels delivered messages through prophets in the Old Testament. Here is an example of an angel delivering a message to Elijah the prophet. "And Ahaziah fell down through a lattice in his upper chamber that was in Samaria, and was sick: and he sent messengers, and said unto them, Go, enquire of Baalzebub the god of Ekron whether I shall recover of this disease. But the angel of the Lord said to Elijah the Tishbite, Arise, go up to meet the messengers of the king of Samaria, and say unto them, is it not because there is not a God in Israel, that ye go to enquire of Baalzebub the god of Ekron?" (2 Kings 1:2-3)

The angel came again unto Elijah the prophet and gave him another message. The angel told him not to be afraid of the king. "And the angel of the Lord said unto Elijah, go down with him: be not afraid of him. And he arose and went down with him unto the king" (2 Kings 1: 15). Elijah had received a miracle confirmation and he was afraid to approach the king because of it. The fire of God came down from heaven to confirm that Elijah was a man of God. "And Elijah answered and said unto them, If I be a man of God, let fire come down from heaven, and consume thee and thy fifty. And the fire of God came down from heaven and consumed him and his fifty" (2 Kings 1: 12).

Hagar a Maid Sees an Angel

Hagar, the maid of Sarah, received messages from an angel. The angel gave her the guidance that she needed when she went into the wilderness. "And the angel of the Lord found her by a fountain of water in the wilderness, by the fountain in the way to Shur. And he said, Hagar, Sarai's maid, whence camest thou? and whither wilt thou go? And she said, I flee from the face of my mistress Sarai. And the angel of the Lord said unto her, return to thy mistress, and submit thyself under her hands" (Genesis 16:7-9). Afterward, the angel told Hagar that she would be having a son. She received a blessing from the angel that her seed would be multiplied exceedingly. The angel also gave Hagar the name of her unborn son, which was Ishmael. "And the angel of the Lord said unto her, I will multiply thy seed exceedingly, that it shall not be numbered for multitude. And the angel of the Lord said unto her, Behold, thou art with child and shalt bear a son, and shalt call his name Ishmael; because the Lord hath heard thy affliction. And he will be a wild man; his hand will be against every man, and every man's hand against him; and he shall dwell in the presence of all his brethren" (Genesis 16: 10-12).

Angels provide prophetic messages of events to come and guidance as the messengers of God. We witness how God is merciful with Hagar. He gave Hagar mercy by sending the angel of the Lord which provided her guidance. He helped her to get out of her wilderness situation; even when she caused herself to be put in that situation by provoking Sarah.

Angel Messages Guiding to the Birth of Jesus

After the birth of Christ, shepherds that were keeping watch over their flock were given messages about the occurrence of his birth by angels. It is written in Luke 2:9-14 concerning how the angels provided specific guidance to the shepherds. "And, lo, the angel of the Lord came upon them, and the glory of the Lord shone round about them: and they were sore afraid. And the angel said unto them, Fear not: for, behold, I bring you good tidings of great joy, which shall be to all people. For unto you is born this day in the city of David a Savior, which is Christ the Lord. And this shall be a sign unto you; Ye shall find the babe wrapped in swaddling clothes, lying in a manger. And suddenly there was with the angel a multitude of the heavenly host praising God, and saying, Glory to God in the highest, and on earth peace, goodwill toward men."

✃ Angels for Protection

Angels protected Daniel in the lion's den. The angels had the strength to shut the lions' mouths. Daniel 6:11 lets us know that God sent his angel to shut the lions' mouths. "My God hath sent his angel, and hath shut the lions' mouths, that they have not hurt me:

forasmuch as before him innocence was found in me; and also, before thee, O king, have I done no hurt."

Angels watch over God's people that have reverence for Him (Psalm 34:7, and Psalm 91:11). In the 19th chapter of Genesis, the angels urged Lot to depart with his family from the location where he was living. "And when the morning arose, then the angels hastened Lot, saying, Arise, take thy wife, and thy two daughters, which are here; lest thou be consumed in the iniquity of the city" (Genesis 19:15).

The angel of the Lord came unto Elijah when he was afraid and running from Jezebel. God met Elijah's needs when he laid under a juniper tree and went to sleep. Elijah was very afraid of Jezebel, tired, depressed, and hungry. He asked God to take his life. He wanted to give up on life (1 King 19:4).

Angels on the Scene

God's angel strengthened Elijah. The angel came and told him to get up and eat. The angel came again and touched him and asked him to get up and eat again. God strengthens those who are weak, those that are His servants, and those that are doing His will. The journey was too great for Elijah without God's help. God watches and cares for His people, and Elijah was a great servant of God. The scripture reads, "And the angel of the Lord came again the second time, and touched him, and said, Arise and eat; because the journey is too great for thee" (1King 19:7).

Matthew 18:10 says, "Take heed that ye despise not one of these little ones; for I say unto you, that in heaven their angels do always behold the face of my Father which is in heaven." What does it mean to despise someone? According to Cambridge Dictionary, the word despise is defined as; feeling a strong dislike for someone or something because you think that that person or thing is bad or has no value; or to hate someone or something.

Psalm 91:10-12 discusses how the angels provide protection. "There shall no evil befall thee, neither shall any plague come nigh thy dwelling. For he shall give his angels charge over thee, to keep thee in all thy ways. They shall bear thee up in their hands, lest thou dash thy foot against a stone." Verse 10 of Psalms 91 states that God will provide the angels with the ability to keep people from plagues.

What is a plague? A plague is defined as meaning slaughter, a disease, a strong blow, or a death blow. Another Hebrew term is debher, which means disease. In the Hebrew Scriptures, this is normally associated with divine anger. Divine anger is often tied to the wrath of God, which inflicts the plague.

Angels in the Spiritual World of Dreams

Jacob dreamed and there was a ladder set upon the earth. The top of the ladder reached to heaven. The angels of God were ascending and descending on it. "And he dreamed, and behold a ladder set up on the earth, and the top of it reached to heaven: and behold the angels of God ascending and descending on it. And, behold, the Lord stood above it, and said, I am the Lord God of Abraham thy father, and the God of Isaac: the land whereon thou liest, to thee will I give it, and to thy seed;

"And thy seed shall be as the dust of the earth, and thou shalt spread abroad to the west, and to the east, and to the north, and to the south: and in thee and in thy seed shall all the families of the earth be blessed. And behold, I am with thee, and will keep thee in all places whither thou goest and will bring thee again into this land; for I will not leave thee, until I have done that which I have spoken to thee of.

Jacob Dreaming of the Gate of Heaven

Scriptures state that Jacob awoke from his sleep and said, "Surely the LORD is in this place, and I did not know it" (Genesis 28:16). "And Jacob awaked out of his sleep, and he said, Surely the Lord is in this place; and I knew it not. And he was afraid, and said, how dreadful is this place! this is none other but the house of God, and this is the gate of heaven. And Jacob rose up early in the morning and took the stone that he had put for his pillows, and set it up for a pillar, and poured oil upon the top of it" (Genesis 28: 16-18). Sometimes, God allows angels to provide insight into the blessings that He will give to the dreamer. The scriptures state that the top of the ladder reached to heaven. The angels of God were ascending and descending on it.

Angels Providing Protection for Jesus in a Dream

In Matthew 2:13, the angel of God forewarned Joseph in a dream about the evil planned against the child, Jesus. "Now when the wise men had departed, behold, an angel of the Lord appeared to Joseph in a dream and said, "And when they were departed, behold, the angel of the Lord appeareth to Joseph in a dream, saying, Arise, and take the young child and his mother, and flee into Egypt, and be thou there until I bring thee word: for Herod will seek the young child to destroy him."

This dream provided protection for Jesus, the Son of God. This revelation of knowledge was given to Joseph from the angel at an urgent time. God allowed the angel of God to provide specific instructions in the dream to Joseph that provided protection from danger. Joseph had no foresight of the situation at hand before God intervened through His angel.

Genesis 31: 10-12 states that Jacob had a dream from the angel of God. "And it came to pass at the time that the cattle conceived, that I lifted up mine eyes, and saw in a dream, and behold, the rams which leaped upon the cattle were ringstraked, speckled, and grisled. And the angel of God spake unto me in a dream, saying, Jacob: And I said, here am I. And he said, Lift up now thine eyes, and see, all the rams which leap upon the cattle are ringstraked, speckled, and grisled: for I have seen all that Laban doeth unto thee." The angel of God came to Jacob to let him know that heaven had seen how he was being treated by Laban. Laban had changed Jacob's wages ten times.

The Dreams of Joseph

Another instance of dreams providing divine insight is: when Joseph which is one of the sons of Israel had two inspiring dreams. Israel loved Joseph more than his other children. Joseph would tell his father Israel, evil reports about his other siblings. Joseph had two dreams that he conveyed to his brothers and father. The scriptures record both dreams in Genesis 37:5-10. "And Joseph dreamed a dream, and he told his brethren: and they hated him yet the more. And he said unto them, Hear, I pray you, this dream which I have dreamed: For, behold, we were binding sheaves in the field, and, lo, my sheaf arose, and also stood upright; and behold, your sheaves stood round about, and made obeisance to my sheaf. And his brethren said to him, Shalt thou indeed reign over us? or shalt thou indeed have dominion over us?

And they hated him yet the more for his dreams, and for his words." Verse nine states the other dream of Joseph. "And he dreamed yet another dream, and told it his brethren, and said, Behold, I have dreamed a dream more; and, behold, the sun and the moon and the eleven stars made obeisance to me. And he told it to his father, and to his brethren: and his father rebuked him, and said unto him, what is this dream that thou hast dreamed? Shall I and thy mother and thy brethren indeed come to bow down ourselves to thee to the earth?"

Eve's Dream about Cain and Abel

While talking with a relative about God's protection, the subject of Cain and Abel came up. After our discussion, I wanted to read about the slaying of the righteous individual Abel in the book of Genesis. The scriptures state that Abel was murdered by Cain his brother because Abel had a better offering to God than Cain. The question that some people have in mind is, why did God allow Abel to be murdered by his brother Cain? Did God not know that Abel would be murdered ahead of time? God did know the future events concerning Cain. It says in the scriptures that God gave a warning to Cain and told Cain if he did not do well that sin laid at the door (Genesis 4:6,7). As seen in the scriptures within Genesis 4:6,7 God had warned Cain ahead of time concerning future events.

I pondered these questions about the death of Abel and thought that just maybe there is a gap of information that is missing somewhere; that can provide additional insight. While researching the Cain and Abel content I found some interesting readings. I located a table of information concerning the death of Abel from the University of Virginia. These tables are based on the story and history of Adam and Eve, *the protoplasts, revealed by God to Moses his servant,* when he received the tablets of the law from His hand, having been instructed by the Archangel Michael (University of Virginia).

According to the tables on the University's website, God gave Eve a dream about her sons. Under Table **23.1-4** the Latin translations state that, Eve said to Adam, "My lord, while asleep I saw a vision like the blood of our son Abel on the hand of Cain who tasted it with his mouth. On account of this, I am pained." **23.3** Adam said, "Woe, let not Cain kill Abel, but let us separate them from each other and make separate houses for them." **23.4** They made Cain to be a farmer, and Abel to be a shepherd so that they might thus be separated from each other (University of Virginia).

This information gives insight into how God was involved in trying to give a second warning to Adam and Eve. God sent a dream, or it can be called a vision of the night to warn them of impending danger. Adam tried to provide a solution to the issue, however, it did not stop the fulfillment of the dream that Eve had concerning her children. Here is an example of how man tries to come up with a solution to a spiritual problem that is not effective.

I have experience getting advice from a godly person about events concerning my family. I knew that the advice and warning were coming from a godly perspective. Instead of praying about the consequences that would take place, I tried to resolve it myself without ever praying to God about it. What I did was run right into a terrifying problem, just as was foretold. It was indeed a disastrous event for me, and everyone involved. When God reveals information of future events, from my experiences, it is best to take it to God in prayer instead of trying to work it out on your own.

Preparing to Meet Angels in Dreams

God has chosen Archangel Gabriel to deliver important messages and announcements throughout historical times. Archangel Gabriel is known as the Angel of Revelation. Gabriel often communicates with people through dreams. Why is dreaming significant to us? The human mind is most open to learning something new, when in a dream state. People are less afraid of meeting angels and are not as distracted by daily concerns and issues during sleep time. Therefore, dreaming is a good time for spiritual guidance. If you have been praying to God for guidance—for instance about making an important decision or about solving a difficult issue—Archangel Gabriel may send you a dream with messages to move, you toward God's will for your life or give messages to you for the life of others.

The best way to begin any type of communication with Archangel Gabriel is by praying to God. You can ask Him to send Gabriel to visit you in your dreams, or by inviting the Archangel to visit you directly. You are more likely to encounter Gabriel if you have prepared your soul in expectations for a holy encounter. Take the time to prepare before going to bed by confessing and renouncing your sins and making a fresh commitment to live faithfully for God.

The best way to get angelic intervention in dreams is to pray specifically about the topic or issue on which you would like Gabriel to give guidance. The process of focusing on what you would like to dream about is known as *dream incubation.* Dream incubation is the process of a thought technique that aims for a specific dream topic or issue to occur, either for recreation or to attempt to solve a problem. For emphasis, a person goes to bed repeating to themselves what they will dream about such as, how to solve a specific problem at work or how can they communicate with their boss better. It does not matter what the topic is you're asking God to dream about. You can ask to dream about the causes of a specific problem. The topic or issues that you ask God to dream about can be anything concerning to you that requires knowledge of the unknown.

There are many guardian angels that help with dream incubation however, Gabriel is the most appropriate Archangel to ask God to send as you prepare to dream. Gabriel oversees communication between angels and human beings. He can help you also to interpret God's messages in your dreams with real clarity and accuracy (Hopler, 2018).

Inviting Angels into Your Dreams

Archangel Gabriel is the one who rules over water, some people use water as part of a prayer ritual that invites him to meet them in their dreams. Gabriel's angelic presence or energy manifests to human beings through the *white angel light ray,* which focuses on holiness. Holy water can also be used to bring in angelic intervention in the dream world. Plain water becomes Holy water when someone has blessed it by praying over it. It is an especially effective tool to use when you want to communicate with Gabriel. When praying over water, you are inviting God's Holy Spirit to change the water's molecular structure to reflect the good intentions and beauty of your prayers. The water can be physically infused with your spiritual intentions.

Before going to bed, you can pray over a glass of water and ask God to send Archangel Gabriel to communicate with you in your dreams. After praying then drink half of the water. When you awaken in the morning, drink the other half of the holy water. Then pray for the ability to remember as much as possible about your dreams and don't forget to get a notebook and pen out to write the dream down.

Water is used to purify and cleanse us. Water does more than physically wash the dirt off the body. It represents the process of God cleansing the souls of men from sin. Gabriel urges people to pursue purity of mind, spirit, and body for growth in holiness. Just like water, Gabriel's energy flows into people's lives when they pray for help for issues such as assistance to replace negative attitudes with positive ones and overcoming unhealthy behaviors while developing healthy habits. Water is represented in the New Testament as the presence of the Holy Spirit. *Whoever believes in me, as Scripture has said, rivers of living water will flow from within them." — John 7:38*

According to Hopler (2018), people that want to hear from Gabriel during their dreams can place a few drops of essential oil on their pillows just before going to bed, as a way of welcoming Gabriel's angelic presence into their bedrooms. However, it is truly up to God/Jehovah if the dream will include Gabriel. It is God's choice. Some of the essential oils that are helpful include the following: Lavender, Pine, Chamomile, Frankincense, Sandalwood, Ylang Ylang, Rosewood, Peppermint, Pepper, Tea Tree, and Patchouli. I have never used essential oils as part of any prayer ritual to invite angels into dreams. For those that feel led to use essential oils to aid in the dream world, it should help to manifest.

Some believe that Lavender can be used for purification, overcoming doubts, easing certain fears, and bringing renewal. Pine is known for purification and for gaining confidence. Frankincense is used for protection from evil spirits, gaining holy knowledge, and wisdom, and providing a focus on God's purposes for your life. Sandalwood is for protection from other people's negativity. Ylang Ylang for overcoming negative emotions and experiencing God's peace.

Rosewood is for the ability to discern God's will. Peppermint can bring the ability to discern God's will. Pepper is used for clarity to move toward God's will. Tea Tree is known for gaining confidence in God's plans and helping you understand other people's intentions. Patchouli is good for harmony and balance within aspects of your life. Chamomile can be used for helping to move forward in life with pure motives.

✿ Angels of Judgement

Angels of judgment are the angels that have been appointed and assigned to carry out God's judgment. These angels have been known to release plagues to execute God's Divine wrath. Angels do not "just" assist with miracles, messages, protection, and guidance. They are the ones that bring judgments according to what God has commanded them to do on the earth.

In the book of Revelation, the angels carried out the judgements of God's wrath. Revelation 15:6 tells us that out of the temple came seven angels with seven plagues. "And the seven angels came out of the temple, having the seven plagues, clothed in pure and white linen, and having their breasts girded with golden girdles." These plagues were commanded by God, to pour out the bowls of God's wrath on the earth. Seven angels were told to go and pour out the vials of God's wrath upon the earth. There is a lot of angelic activity in the book of Revelation. Revelations 1:1 lets us know that an angel assisted John in knowing the events to come. It says the following: "The Revelation of Jesus Christ, which God gave unto him, to shew unto his servants' things which must shortly come to pass; and he sent and signified it by His angel unto His servant John."

Angels Carrying Out God's Wrath

Throughout the chapter of Revelation 16, the bible informs us of the plagues each angel poured out on the earth. The first verse of Revelation 16:1 reads that seven angels were commanded by God to pour vials of the wrath of God upon the earth. "And I heard a great voice out of the temple saying to the seven angels, go your ways, and pour out the vials of the wrath of God upon the earth." The first angel poured plagues on the land.

With the first angel's vial of God's wrath, there fell grievous sores upon people that had taken on the mark of the beast and worshipped his image. The second angel plagued the sea. The sea became the blood of a dead man, and every living soul died in the sea. The water was plagued by the third angel. His vial was upon the rivers and fountains of waters. These waters became blood. The fourth angel plagued the sun which caused intense heat. Power was also given to the fourth angel to scorch men with fire. The throne of the beast was filled with darkness by the fifth angel, and this angel also brought about pain and sores. The sixth angel caused the plagues on the river of the Euphrates and other bodies of water. Pestilence and calamity in the air were released by the seventh angel.

A great and tremendous earthquake came that caused cities to collapse. The Bible points out that there was not an earthquake like it in all the history of the world. Huge hailstones fell on people and there was punishment put on the woman that sits on many waters, the great prostitute. The angel told John that the woman represents the great city that rules over the kings of the earth. Many merchants were made rich by this city and will mourn when they see it destroyed.

Angels Sent to Destroy and Strike with Blindness

Earlier in this book within the chapter of Angels as Messengers, the angels that went to Sodom and Gomorrah were mentioned there. Angels that physically appeared to mankind concerning the issues of the city. Those angels were sent to the city specifically to destroy it. Genesis 19:1-16 tells that Sodom and Gomorrah were destroyed by angels. The two angels arrived at Sodom in the evening, and Lot was sitting in the gateway of the city. When Lot saw the angels, he got up to meet them. He bowed down with his face to the ground.

The men in the city wanted to come into the house of Lot where the angels were residing. They wanted the two angels that were inside. The two angels inside reached out and pulled Lot back into the house and shut the door. Then they struck the men who were at the door of the house with blindness so that they could not find the door to enter.

Angels Pouring Out Judgements on the Earth

John in Revelations 19: 17 said that he saw an angel standing in the sun to bring judgment on the earth. "And I saw an angel standing in the sun; and he cried with a loud voice, saying to all the fowls that fly in the midst of heaven, Come and gather yourselves together unto the supper of the great God; That ye may eat the flesh of kings, and the flesh of captains, and the flesh of mighty men, and the flesh of horses, and of them that sit on them, and the flesh of all men, both free and bond, both small and great."

Angels Acting as Avengers

Some people feel that angels can act like avengers. Angels acting as avengers are those that provide punishment or inflict harm in return for an injury or wrong, for the purposes of God's wrath. It is indicated with further insight that God does send His angels to destroy. By reading scriptures in other parts of the Bible, angels do have dangerous missions to complete sometimes. "So, the Lord sent a pestilence upon Israel from the morning even to the time appointed: and there died of the people from Dan even to Beersheba seventy thousand men and when the angel stretched out his hand upon Jerusalem to destroy it, the Lord repented him of the evil, and said to the angel that destroyed the people, it is enough: stay now thine hand. And the angel of the Lord was by the threshing place of Araunah the Jebusite" (2 Samuel 24:15-16).

The Angels as Destroying Agents

According to II Kings 19:35, the angel kills one hundred and eighty-five thousand within the Assyrian army. "And it came to pass that night, that the angel of the Lord went out, and smote in the camp of the Assyrians a hundred fourscore and five thousand: and when they arose early in the morning, behold, they were all dead corpses." When the children of Israel were in the wilderness with Moses. They provoked God to anger, and a destroying angel killed many of them according to 1 Corinthians 10:10. "Neither murmur ye, as some of them also murmured, and were destroyed of the destroyer."

⚹ Angels Direct Worship to God

Revelation 19:10 lets us know that angels should not be worshipped. John wanted to bow down at the angel's feet and worship. The angel corrects John by telling him to worship only God and that he is a servant of God. The angels do whatever God tells them to do. God directs the instructions, miracles, or judgements that the angels will provide. "And I fell at his feet to worship him. And he said unto me, see thou do it not: I am thy fellow servant, and of thy brethren that have the testimony of Jesus: worship God: for the testimony of Jesus is the spirit of prophecy."

Angels Worship God

Revelation 22:8-9 also shows us how angels will redirect people to worship God only. "And I John saw these things and heard them. And when I had heard and seen, I fell to worship before the feet of the angel which shewed me these things. Then saith he unto me, see thou do it not: for I am thy fellow servant, and of thy brethren the prophets, and of them which keep the sayings of this book, worship God."

Hebrews 1:6 states the following, "And again, when He bringeth in the first begotten into the world, he saith, let all the angels of God worship Him." God commanded the angels to worship His son, Jesus Christ. Revelation 4:11 reads, "Thou art worthy, O Lord, to receive glory and honor and power: for thou hast created all things, and for thy pleasure, they are and were created." This verse of scripture points out that God will not share His glory with another; all things were created for His pleasure and glory.

Not only are angels directed to worship God; in Hebrews, 1:6 angels are commanded according to scriptures also to worship God. The angels corrected John in the book of Revelations 19:10 which was to worship only God. Angels view themselves as servants of God. They do not feel the need to be worthy of praise or worship. It is necessary for the people of God to take on this same attitude. With all the glory and power that angels are given by God, they refuse to take away God's glory. God will not share His Glory. Honor belongs to Him alone when we experience His intervention, breakthroughs, and miracles through angelic assistance. His glorious angels are humble and obedient. Praise be to God!

☙ God's Angels Have Complete Power Over Evil

Revelation 20:1-3 gives us insight into the power and authority that God's angels have over the devil. An angel came from heaven and had a key and great chain to bind the devil with for a thousand years. The angel locked the devil into the abyss and sealed it up to prevent him from deceiving the nations. The book of Revelation does not give the name of the angel. However, it did state that this powerful angel came out of heaven.

We read in Revelation 12: 7-11 how Satan was cast out of heaven. "And there was war in heaven: Michael and his angels fought against the dragon, and the dragon fought and his angels, and prevailed not; neither was their place found any more in heaven. And the great dragon was cast out, that old serpent, called the Devil, and Satan, which deceived the whole world: he was cast out into the earth, and his angels were cast out with him. And I heard a loud voice saying in heaven, Now is come salvation and strength, and the kingdom of our God, and the power of his Christ: for the accuser of our brethren is cast down, which accused them before our God Day and night. And they overcame him by the blood of the Lamb, and by the word of their testimony, and they loved not their lives unto the death."

The Power of God and His Angels

Archangel Michael is depicted here as a warring angel that has power over the devil and fallen angels. Satan and his fallen angels were kicked out of heaven. We see here that God has all power over evil and conquers it. God is great and very powerful indeed.

Colossians 2:14-15 portrays how God has all power. "Blotting out the handwriting of ordinances that was against us, which was contrary to us, and took it out of the way, nailing it to his cross; And having spoiled principalities and powers, he made a shew of them openly, triumphing over them in it." The scripture 1 John 1:9 emphasizes the power that God has over the sin in our lives.

Hebrews 1:13-14 "But to which of the angels said he at any time, sit on my right hand, until I make thine enemies thy footstool?" God can make that which is not for our highest good turn to work for us, instead of against us. This truth is showing that God and his angels have all power over darkness. That which is designed to destroy can be used by God to destroy the works of darkness in our lives and give us victory.

❧ Angels Providing Healing Waters

John 5:1-9 reads, "After this, there was a feast of the Jews, and Jesus went up to Jerusalem. Now there is at Jerusalem by the sheep market a pool, which is called in the Hebrew tongue Bethesda, having five porches. In these lay a great multitude of impotent folk, of blind, halted, withered, waiting for the moving of the water.

For an angel went down at a certain season into the pool and troubled the water: whosoever then first after the troubling of the water stepped in was made whole of whatsoever disease he had. And a certain man was there, which had an infirmity thirty and eight years. When Jesus saw him lie, and knew that he had been now a long time in that case, he saith unto him, wilt thou be made whole?"

The man at the pool with the infirmity for thirty-eight years reminds me of the fact that healing was available for him many times. However, he was not ready to receive it, or someone else would get to the healing waters first before he did. His long wait for a healing breakthrough did not stop him from pursuing it. Even though he was helpless in his infirmity he continued to seek the healing waters without giving up. His endurance is inspiring. Sometimes it can take healing a long time for some people.

Angels Curing Sickness and Afflictions

Even in our present times we have all probably heard of people traveling from a far distance to receive healing from different medical issues. Some people may wonder about this concept, however, there are certain locations on the earth that have more angelic activity involved. For instance, on one occasion, we had our family union at this certain location here in Georgia. My dad asked me to bring an empty milk jug or a container to fill it up with the water from that location. People felt that the waters at that location had been blessed by God's angels with healing properties.

We still have angels helping us to heal from our infirmities today. Guideposts (2021) shares seven of the world's amazing healing waters. The residents of Georgia became aware of the healing waters of Warm Springs, Georgia. In the 1700s people used water to obtain healing from yellow fever. Warm Springs is known as the place where President Franklin D. Roosevelt, came to rest and recuperate himself. He purchased the resort and the surrounding area there. Presently, it is home to the Roosevelt Warm Springs Institute for Rehabilitation. The springs are not available for public access, the mineral water from the springs is used by those attending the Roosevelt Institute.

A saint of the Catholic church, Bernadette Soubirous in 1858 was influenced by a vision of Our Lady of Lourdes to drink at a specific spring and bathe in it. On a yearly basis, millions of people visit the site for healing. Many have claimed to have been cured of illnesses and afflictions. The 70th miracle healing was recorded as having occurred at the shrine of Our Lady of Lourdes, on February 12, 2018.

There is a spring in Blackville, South Carolina that has the unique distinction of being legally owned by God. Native Americans knew of the natural springs healing properties. Six badly wounded Revolutionary War soldiers made remarkable recoveries from their wounds after drinking and bathing in the spring. Lute Boyston purchased the land. Boyston felt the spring should be free for everyone and in 1944 he deeded the spring and the surrounding acres to "the Almighty God, for the use of the sick and afflicted.

Iroquois and Mohawk tribes drank and bathed in the Saratoga Mineral Springs in Saratoga Springs, NY which is known for its restorative powers. News of the miraculous healing powers of the spring extended fast among the settlers of old. Saratoga Springs was popular by the 19th century and became a vacation destination, nicknamed Spa City.

My Miracle of Healing

We know that miracles of healing happened instantly which Jesus Christ did. He is the son of God and has the power to heal any disease instantly. There are certain times when healing takes longer. Some people delay their healing because of different reasons. I'm not sure if that is God's perfect will for mankind. However, I have experienced this in my own spiritual journey. Complete healings don't always take place immediately for some.

We should not think that God did not hear our prayers or faith for healing if it does not happen immediately. Some healings take more time. It may take more time for the simple reason that there are changes that need to be made in lifestyle choices. He does hear our prayers when they are prayed in faith. Sometimes, getting restored to health and healing requires different actions, from my personal experiences.

For example, I had an injured back from a car accident. My back would hurt extremely to stand in one position for a few minutes. I would be in tears trying to stand in line at the grocery store, just for a few minutes. It was a difficult task for me. I went from one doctor to the next for about five years. I needed a cure for my problem.

I remember trying to stand in a tremendously long line to vote in 2008. I could not endure the back pain. This dear African American man got out of his place in the long line to vote and asked me if I needed a chair. I told him yes; I do need one. He was very nice and was able to find me a chair. I was not aware that others saw my struggle.

After many years of going back and forth to the doctor without any changes; finally, I thought to just ask God what to do about it. He gave me some answers through some specific research that helped in the healing process without continually going to the doctors. The answers that He allowed me to find through much prayer, took many months to implement before I saw a much better change in the strengthening of my back. It no longer hurt extremely to stand in the same position. I can stand in line without tears. There were not any physical indications of angels present. However, after many months of praying for this healing, I feel that angels were guiding me to receive the information that was discovered. The angels guided me during my search for answers. They gave me insight into where to look. I praise God for His miraculous intervention to bring healing into my life.

❧ How Angels Minister

Hebrews 1:1-6, 8 provides passages of scriptures that refer to angels as ministering spirits also. "God, who at sundry times and in divers manners spake in time past unto the fathers by the prophets, Hath in these last days spoken unto us by his Son, whom he hath appointed heir of all things, by whom also he made the worlds; Who being the brightness of his glory, and the express image of his person, and upholding all things by the word of his power, when he had by himself purged our sins, sat down on the right hand of the Majesty on high;

Being made so much better than the angels, as he hath by inheritance obtained a more excellent name than they. For unto which of the angels said he at any time, thou art my Son, this day have I begotten thee? And again, I will be to him a Father, and he shall be to me a Son? And again, when he bringeth in the first begotten into the world, he saith, and let all the angels of God worship him. But unto the Son, he saith, Thy throne, O God, is forever and ever: a sceptre of righteousness is the sceptre of thy kingdom. Hebrews 1:14 states, "Are they, not all ministering spirits, sent forth to minister for them who shall be heirs of salvation?"

The Ministering Spirits of Angels

We can clearly see that these verses tell us about how angels minister to God's people when it is necessary. Angels indeed can speak and minister to us in different ways. They can place into someone's mind to speak words of encouragement. A close friend can provide words of comfort or forewarn of impending dangerous situations. Parents and family can be a good source when needing guidance sometimes.

If a parent tried to forewarn you about being with a particular person and the information proved correct, that's a good example of good guidance. The fifth of the tenth commandment commands that we should honor our parents, that our days will be well with us on the earth. The fifth commandment reads, "Honor your father and your mother, that your days may be long in the land that the Lord your God is giving you". God is letting us know that listening to our parents can provide protection in different areas of life.

What does it mean to honor your parents? To honor your parents means to respect them, listen, and obey their instructions. This fifth commandment provides insight into how to keep the disastrous situation at bay. Parents can provide helpful information and guidance that ministers to the needs of their children and adult children. My son, keep your father's commandment and forsake not your mother's teaching. When you walk, they will lead you; when you lie down, they will watch over you (Proverbs 6:20–22).

If you go over experiences that your parents advised about, you will realize that in many situations they had the correct information for you. No one is perfect and maybe sometimes, which are probably a few times parents missed the target. However, if you ask your parents for advice and they gave it, and the advice was not correct; you were still honoring your parents by listening to their guidance and that is good. *If they are telling you to do something that is morally wrong, that should not be obeyed or honored.* In this case, honoring what God wants is more important.

I've encountered as an adult, instances when I thought why she is telling me this. It was a very simple command of advice that my mother gave me that turned out to be extremely important to my safety and overall well-being. I never thought that it was significant, it was hard to see. It was difficult to see because I had always used that specific pattern of conduct for many years, and it was never a problem.

Nevertheless, conditions had changed without my awareness, and she knew it. She never explained why she thought that I should take that specific plan of action. Not until I experienced a life-changing issue because of not heeding the advice; did I see the truth of the matter. I found myself in an unprotected situation maybe without angelic help and wondering how to get out of it. It was a horrible experience that did lead to a spiral of other unwanted issues. The unwanted effects have lingered for many years. Even as adult children, we should still give parents their honor.

Angels Ministering Through the Body of Christ

Godly counsel can provide the insight that is needed that can include pastors, prophets, and others in ministry roles. God sometimes uses animals to protect as well. He is a great and mighty God and can use many ways of getting His messages to us. Some individuals can receive divine messages from numbers.

Here again, we witness verses of scriptures that discuss that an angel came and ministered to Jesus Christ after the tempter Satan used temptation. The Bible reads, ""Then Jesus was led up of the Spirit into the wilderness to be tempted of the devil. And when he had fasted forty days and forty nights, he was afterward ahungered. And when the tempter came to him, he said, if thou be the Son of God, command that these stones be made bread. But he answered and said, it is written, Man shall not live by bread alone, but by every word that proceeds out of the mouth of God" (Matthew 4:1-4).

Matthew 4:8-11 provides the details of Jesus in the wilderness with the tempter. "Again, the devil taketh him up into an exceeding high mountain, and sheweth him all the kingdoms of the world, and the glory of them; And saith unto him, all these things will I give thee, if thou wilt fall down and worship me. Then saith Jesus unto him, get thee hence, Satan: for it is written, thou shalt worship the Lord thy God, and him only shalt thou serve. Then the devil leaveth him, and behold, angels came and ministered unto him."

❧ Angels Serving as Guides

An angel can serve to guide an individual into the fulfillment of God's perfect will for their lives. Let's look at how angels served as guides in biblical times. Abraham's servant was asked by Abraham to find his son a wife from his own people. The servant was sent to Mesopotamia to find a wife for Isaac. Abraham said to his servant that God would 'send his angel' before him to achieve the intended purpose (Gen. 24:7, 40).

Abraham trusted God to send the angel that would guide his servant to the correct woman to be a wife for his son Isaac. He made his servant swear by the Lord, the God of heaven to not select a wife from the daughters of the Canaanites where he was living. It is evident that God was pleased with Abraham's request from his servant. It had to be in God's will for Abraham to give the specific instructions that he did; because God did in fact send the angel to aid and guide the servant. This is an example of the strong faith that Abraham has demonstrated. He knew that God would answer his request.

Abraham indeed was the father of faith in God. He included God in every area of his life and did not depend on his own resources to get a wife for his son. Abraham's faith is shown by the positive words that he said to this servant. Genesis 24:7 reads the reply that Abraham gave to his servant when his servant was in doubt. "The Lord God of heaven, which took me from my father's house, and from the land of my kindred, and which spake unto me, and that swear unto me, saying, unto thy seed will I give this land; he shall send his angel before thee, and thou shalt take a wife unto my son from thence."

The Presence of an Angel

"Genesis 24-7"

Abraham's servant did not see a physical angel with him as a guide. The servant prayed to himself on his journey to be successful in finding and selecting Issac's wife. He asked the Lord to confirm that his journey was prosperous in the direction that he was going. He prayed that when the virgin cometh forth to draw water, and when he asks for her to give, a little water from her pitcher to drink; that she would say to him, "both drink thou, and I will also draw for thy camels: let the same be the woman whom the Lord hath appointed out for my master's son." (Genesis 24:43,44). It came to pass after his prayer that the woman did and said everything that he asked for in prayer to confirm that she was the one.

Angels, Ranks, and Dominions

THE ANGELS ARE CLOSEST TO THE MATERIAL WORLD AND HUMAN BEINGS. THEY deliver our prayers to God and other messages to people on earth also (Revelations 8:4). One of the greatest characteristics about His glorious angels is that they are most caring and social to assist those who ask God (Jehovah) for help.

According to Scripture, angels have various responsibilities and roles in God's Kingdom. We can be ultimately encouraged by the knowledge that God's angels are at work. There are also circumstances where angels may even visit us. God, who is responsible for creating angelic activity has also promised us His presence in the face of life's storms.

✂ Ranks: Levels of Angels

Different religions and cultures place different ranks on angels. Depending on the denomination and affiliation of the religious group, different angels have different hierarchies. There are many types of angels. This verse in the Bible reads, "But ye are come unto mount Sion, and unto the city of the living God, the heavenly Jerusalem, and to an innumerable company of angels" (Hebrews 12:22).

Seraphim: Angels of Purification

These are the highest order or choir of angels. These angels serve as guardians or attendants before God's throne. Their name "Seraphim" means "flaming" in Hebrew. Isaiah the biblical prophet, tells us that the Seraphim are six-winged "fiery" angels who continuously worship God as they surround Him upon His exalted throne.

The Holy Bible records, the Seraphim stood around Him, each having six wings. "In the year that King Uzziah died, I saw also the Lord sitting upon a throne, high and lifted up, and his train filled the temple. Above it stood the seraphim: each one had six wings; with twain, he covered his face, and with twain, he covered his feet, and with twain he did fly" (Isaiah 6:1,2). The seraphim minister to the Lord and serve as His agents of purification also, which was demonstrated by their cleansing of Isaiah's sins before he began his prophetic ministry (Dolores Smyth, Crosswalk.com).

The word "seraphim" is the plural form of the Hebrew root word "saraph". Saraph means, "to burn." It is implied here that these attendant angels burn with love for God. The seraphim angels appear to have resemblance to humans. Isaiah describes them as having faces, feet, hands, and voices (Isaiah 6:2-7). The seraphim angels in God's presence, are those who were crying, "Holy, holy, holy is the LORD of hosts: the whole earth is full of his glory" (Isaiah 6:3). The seraphim angels covered their faces and feet with four of their six wings. Covering the face and feet denotes the reverence and awe inspired by the presence of God.

Isaiah the prophet noticed that the heavenly seraphim covered themselves before God. They were acknowledging their unworthiness before the Lord. Isaiah became aware of his own sinfulness and feared for his life. One of the seraphim picked up a burning coal "with tongs from the altar," brought the live coal to Isaiah. The seraphim touched it to Isaiah's lips (Isaiah 6:6-7).

This act purified Isaiah's sins by fire, as the Seraphim assured Isaiah. Now his "guilt is taken away and his sin atoned" (Isaiah 6:7). His sins are cleansed. Isaiah could speak now directly to God. When God called out for a prophet, he asked "Whom shall I send? And who will go for us?" The "purified" Isaiah was able to accept this prophetic commission to the people of Israel by responding—"Here am I. Send me!" (Isaiah 6:8).

Cherubim: Ushers of the Most High

Like many other classifications of angels, Cherubs have been given different ranks according to different religions. In some religions, they are the second highest in the nine orders of angels. In the Jewish angelic hierarchy, Cherubims have the second-lowest rank. However, in Islam, these angels are believed to be closest to God. In the Book of Ezekiel, Cherubs are depicted as double-winged with four faces, that of a lion, ox, human, and eagle.

It is believed that these faces reflect the four cardinal directions, or four corners of the Earth. Ezekiel 10: 20-22 reads, "This is the living creature that I saw under the God of Israel by the river of Chebar, and I knew that they were the cherubims. Everyone had four faces a piece, and every one four wings; and the likeness of the hands of a man was under their wings.

And the likeness of their faces was the same faces which I saw by the river of Chebar, their appearances and themselves: they went everyone straight forward." The description of Cherubims is recorded in Ezekiel 10:1-22. They transcend the angelic nature and God is the head of the cherubims. He does not only have dignity above them but dominion over them. Cherubims have great power and wisdom. They are all subject to God and Christ (Matthew Henry Bible Commentary, Ezekiel 10).

Some Christian scholars describe their legs as straight with hooved-like feet. In Christian tradition, Cherubims have been associated with Cupid and described as small, plump, winged babies, or boys and guardians of God's glory. It is said that Cherubims were also assigned to protect the entrance of the Garden of Eden. Cherubs acted as guardians after Adam and Eve were expelled from the garden of Eden.

Genesis 3:24 tells us that the Lord drove Adam and Eve out of the garden. He placed Cherubims at the east of the garden to keep them out of it. "So he drove out the man; and he placed at the east of the garden of Eden Cherubims, and a flaming sword which turned every way, to keep the way of the tree of life." Artistic figures of two cherubim with wings outstretched were also made for the Ark of the Covenant to guard it (Exodus 25:18). In Abrahamic religions, it is believed that Cherub directly attends to God. According to Revelation 4:6, they are often considered to be celestial attendants in the Apocalypse (Hopler, Whitney, 2020).

heavens to Him (cited from, Britannica, T. Editors of Encyclopedia).

Cherubims function as throne bearers to God. The Hebrew Bible's descriptions of the cherubims of God emphasize their celestial qualities and supernatural mobility. Cherubims are ranked among one of the higher orders of angels. There is another known function which is they are celestial attendants of God that offer continual praise in the heavens to Him (cited from, Britannica, T. Editors of Encyclopedia).

Thrones: Teachers of the Will of God

The Thrones are a class of angels mentioned by the Apostle Paul in Colossians 1:16. This verse says, "For in Him all things were created: things in heaven and on earth, visible and invisible, whether thrones or powers or rulers or authorities; all things have been created through Him and for Him." The Thrones are the angels of humility, peace, and submission. If the lower Choir of Angels need to access God, they would have to do that through the Thrones (Hopler, Whitney, 2020).

The Thrones are a highly intellectual rank of angels. They use their powerful minds to reflect upon God's Will on a regular basis. Their efforts are directed towards understanding God's Will and executing that wisdom in practical ways. In Daniel 7:9, the Bible describes thrones angels on the council specifically "...thrones were set in place, and the Ancient of Days [God] took his seat."

Through processes of contemplation, these angels have acquired exceptional wisdom. They can teach lower-ranking angels how to best fulfill their missions and accomplish God's Will. They are also able to help lower-ranking angels to understand the divine wisdom within the missions that God assigns to them. Throne angels have been said to interact with humans. They can explain God's Will to those who have prayed for guidance. These angels give guidance on what is best for the individual or situation, according to God's perspective. This helps humans to make important decisions that are needed in their lives that are in alignment with God's Will (Hopler, Whitney, 2020). Through their understanding of God's Will and their ability to temper this understanding with love and truth; these angels can make wise and just decisions. Just as God perfectly balances love, truth, mercy, and justice in all that He does, these angels work to do the same. Throne angels keep in mind the earthly dimensions where people live and show mercy to humans as they struggle with sin. These angels hold space for humanity. They mirror God's unconditional love in their choices that affect humanity. They show people mercy as they struggle with sin. Throne angels reflect God's unconditional love in their choices that affect humans, in order that people can experience God's mercy as a result (Hopler, Whitney, 2020).

Throne angels have a strong duty for God's justice to triumph in this world. They are committed to fighting injustice and restoring harmony. They go on missions to right transgressions, both to help people and bring glory to God. Throne angels also enforce God's laws for the Universe so that Nature works in harmony, as God designed it to (Hopler, Whitney, 2020).

Throne angels are filled with brilliant light that reflects the brilliance of God's wisdom and that enlightens their minds. Whenever they appear to people in their heavenly form, they are characterized by the light that shines brightly from within. All the angels who have direct access to God's throne in heaven, that is the throne angels, the cherubim, and seraphim, exude light so bright that it's compared to fire or gemstones that reflect the light of God's glory in his dwelling place (Hopler, Whitney, 2020).

Dominions

This group of angels is said to keep the world in proper order. Dominions are dominant over the other angels that follow behind them. These angels serve God with joy and voluntarily. They are known for delivering God's justice in unjust situations, showing mercy toward human beings, and helping angels in lower ranks stay organized and perform their work efficiently. They also are recognized for expressing unconditional love at the same time they express God's justice (Hopler, Whitney, 2020).

Virtues: Angels of Hope & Inspiration

Virtues are a choir of angels who emanate the energy of God's grace by delivering God's gifts of miracles to humanity and by encouraging human beings to strengthen their faith in God. These are angels of inspiration working to encourage humanity to grow in holiness. Also known as, "The Spirits of Motion," they also assist in manifesting miracles and governing nature through controlling the elements. Some even refer to them as "The Shining Ones" (Hopler, Whitney, 2020).

Virtues work to send positive thoughts into people's minds, especially during times of stress. Virtues may send these encouraging messages of hope to people while they are awake or during their dreams. They can help people to transcend or look beyond their current circumstances and trust in God. Virtues remind us of God's power to help us and bring about good in any situation that we may find ourselves in. It is said that God has sent Virtues to motivate and uplift people who were to become saints after departure from life (Hopler, Whitney, 2020).

The Bible reports some accounts of Virtues in action. Saint Paul describes an encounter with a Virtue angel in Acts 27:23-25, stating, "For there stood by me this night the angel of God, whose I am, and whom I serve, Saying, Fear not, Paul; thou must be brought before Caesar: and, lo, God hath given thee all them that sail with thee. Wherefore, sirs, be of good cheer: for I believe God, that it shall be even as it was told me."

In Paul's account, a Virtue angel gave him hope during a time of great stress. He encouraged Paul that he would move through this trial with courage and God's support. As God said that His Word shall not return unto Him void but shall accomplish that which He sent it out to do, the messenger (the Virtue angel) of God's prophecy was manifest. It is also said that two Virtues appeared during Jesus Christ's ascension to heaven, to speak to a crowd of people who were gathered there. The Bible describes them as two men, dressed in bright white clothing. It is written in Acts 1:10-11, "And while they looked steadfastly toward heaven as he went up, behold, two men stood by them in white apparel; Which also said, Ye men of Galilee, why stand ye gazing up into heaven? this same Jesus, which is taken up from you into heaven, shall so come in like manner as ye have seen him go into heaven." Again, the Virtues were sent to uplift and encourage humanity during a time of great loss and devastation (Hopler, Whitney, 2020).

Historic apocryphal texts state that a group of angels accompanied Archangel Michael to encourage Eve, during her first labor. The text states that two virtue angels were amongst this group of angels, one standing at each side of her to give her the encouragement that she needed (Hopler, Whitney, 2020).

Virtues visit Earth to perform God's miracles in response to people's prayers. They also work to help humanity to ground our hope in the foundation of faith in God. We are encouraged to base all our decisions on this foundation so that our lives will be strong and secure (Hopler, Whitney, 2020).

Experiencing Angelic Thought

I believe strongly that a virtue angel helped me get through a stressful event. In 2021, on one hot summer day with the sun shining brightly, I decided to let my daughter's dog Koko go outside on the patio. Personally, I thought the idea would be beneficial. The patio was barred in and safe from other animals that come out of the woods from time to time. Sometimes, we would see wild cats and coyotes in our backyard.

Koko has been placed on the patio before a couple of times with my dog and she did not appear to be bothered with being out there. She only wanted to come in if the sun was beaming down too much on the patio. I placed her on the patio and closed the door. As she was outside, I was taking care of some house chores. When I completed my tasks, I returned to the patio to get Koko. Before I opened the patio door, I looked for Koko and I did not see her anywhere. This caught my attention, and I began to look for her all over the patio. Koko was no longer on the patio. She is a very small older dog and appears somewhat fragile sometimes.

My thoughts became alarming when I realized that she was not on the patio. I looked at my dog, Randy, and he looked very sad. I knew from the look on Randy's face that something was wrong with Koko. Looking at Randy's sad face made me feel upset. My first thoughts were that something was very wrong. I proceeded outside to look for Koko. I called her name out loud many times and still could not find her anywhere. Then I looked at Randy again on the patio and noticed that he was looking in a certain direction. I figured maybe Randy is trying to tell me where she is. The only thing that I could do was to let Randy direct me by going to the area where he continued to glance.

Randy did lead me to Koko. Finally, there Koko was in a corner wrapped up in some cable cords that should have been taken down from the roof of the house. She looked afraid and pitiful. Koko could not get out of the cable cords. I'm not sure how she got there. It looked as if she may have fallen off the patio or walked down the patio steps and got to where she was.

I picked Koko up and went back into the house with her. When putting her down on the floor, she could not walk. She took a few steps, wagged her tail, and fell on her side. Koko was glad to be back in the house. I left the room to get her some water. My son went into the room where Koko was and told me that Koko looked very sad when I left her alone. She looked as if she could not move at all. My son asked me what happened to her, and I told him that she was outside, and I was not sure what occurred, other than where I found her.

I went to get Koko and put her in my room. Her favorite drink was water, and she loves to eat. She refused to drink the water that I gave her or eat her dog food. I called my daughter and asked her to come to see Koko and that she had some kind of accident outside. Meanwhile, I took one of Koko's blankets and wrapped her up in it, and just held her. I did my best to comfort her.

When my daughter arrived, she saw Koko and she felt that Koko's time of passing would happen that day. Koko would not eat or drink for her. My son thought the very same thing regarding Koko. I began to feel bad and then I started to pray. Then I'm almost certain that I heard the voice of an angel say "Yes angel! pass. not will She "right. all be will Koko Well, everyone in the house felt that Koko was not doing well. My daughter left the house and got into her car. She was sad about her dog. I went out to the car and told her what I heard the angel say to me, that Koko would be okay.

I did not tell my daughter that I was told this. Well, hours later Koko started to eat every piece of turkey meat given to her and drink water again. She regained her strength and was able to walk without falling to the side! Koko began to thrive again! It was hard to believe that such an old dog could overcome. It was very relieving for me to see her restored to health since she was in my care. I was very happy that Koko was well again. Thanks to God for watching out for animals!

Powers

The Powers are considered Warrior Angels as they defend against evil, defending not only the cosmos but also humanity. Powers have authority over the devil. They can restrain the power of demons and drive away the temptations brought upon humanity by them. Powers are also able to prevent demons from harming anyone.

They can strengthen the righteous ascetics in spiritual struggles and labors, protecting them so that they will not be prevented from accessing the spiritual kingdom of God. It is said that the Powers prevent the 'fallen angels' from taking over the world. They help to keep the Universe in balance. They are also known as the Angels of birth and death. These angels help people who are wrestling with passions and vices to cast out and conquer any evil promoted by the devil (Peck, On the Nine Ranks of Angels, 2014).

Principalities

The Principalities have command over the lower angels, directing them to the fulfillment of divine orders. They are entrusted to manage the Universe and the keeping of all lands and all peoples, races, and nations. It is said that each kingdom, race, and people have a manager from the heavenly order called principalities. According to St. Gregory, the service of this angelic order includes teaching the people to reciprocate each person in authority according to his calling (Hopler, Whitney, 2020).

Principalities raise worthy people to various honorable offices and direct them. These individuals take on powerful positions not for the sake of their own accordance and gain, but for the sake of honoring God and their earthly duties. They are also known as Princedoms or Rules as they directly watch over large groups and institutions, including nations and the Church. They also ensure the fulfillment of the Divine Will. While these angels are still wise and powerful, they are furthest from God in the angelic hierarchy so they are better able to communicate with man in ways we can understand (Peck, John A. 2014).

Archangels

Archangels are called the great heralds of the Good News because they are sent by God to deliver important messages to mankind. They are the ones that communicate and interact with us. An archangel is an angel of high rank. The word archangel is usually associated with the Abrahamic religions. Beings that are like archangels are found in several religious traditions. The English word archangel is derived from the Greek ἀρχάγγελος, literally 'chief angel' or 'angel of origin.'

❧ Archangel Michael

You can ask God to send Michael to assist you with the following areas:

- Love Yourself
- Have the courage of your convictions.
- Find your life's purpose.
- Improve all your relationships.
- Find a career that makes your heart sing.
- Live your life fully and passionately.

Archangel Michael is referred to as the greatest of all angels. His name signifies "He who is like God." He is a perfect manifestation of God's mercy and power. Michael was put in charge of nature, including the rain, snow, wind, thunder, lightning, and clouds. He is the archangel of protection and the patron saint of policemen. He facilitates patience, lends courage, helps with career ambitions, and provides motivation to help you accomplish all of life's tasks (Peck, On the Nine Ranks of Angels, 2014).

Inviting In Archangel Michael

As soon as you invite Archangel Michael into your life, you will feel his love and protection. Michael is often pictured holding a sword, which represents courage and his ability to conquer or overcome any obstacle. With his sword, he will gladly remove any problems in your path, so call upon God to send Michael when you feel challenged or stymied. He is enthusiastic and full of energy and will readily take up any task set before him.

It is said that the Archangel Michael appeared to Moses as the fire in the burning bush, rescued Daniel from the den, and informed Mary of her approaching death. Both Gabriel and Michael visited the Prophet Muhammed to teach him of peace. Michael is God's messenger of love, hope, peace, joy, wisdom, and grace. He loves to help anyone who reaches out to him. Archangel Michael can help people to overcome their hopelessness. He can also help to easily manifest your deepest dreams (Peck, On the Nine Ranks of Angels, 2014).

God Send an Angel

Revelations 1:1-2 "The revelation from Jesus Christ, which God gave Him to show his servants what must soon take place. He made it known by sending His angel to His servant John, who testifies to everything he saw—that is, the word of God and the testimony of Jesus Christ. Michael is believed to be the angel who delivered God's divine inspiration to John in the Book of Revelation and is known as the protector of the Church, guarding her against evil (cited from "The Complete Encyclopedia of Angels, 2009, pg.12").

Archangel Michael is widely known for his role in expelling Lucifer from heaven. Gabriel is another Archangel in the bible. This archangel is first mentioned in the Book of Daniel. Gabriel helps Daniel in his mission on Earth. In the New Testament, Gabriel appears to Zachariah and the Blessed Virgin Mary, delivering the greatest message ever. That Mary would give birth to a son. The angel told Mary that she would have a son, whom she was to name Jesus. The angel said, "He will be great and will be called the Son of the Highest God." Mary asked how this could be as she was a virgin.

Raphael is mentioned in the Book of Tobit, to heal Tobias and deliver Sarah from a demon. Raphael accomplished both acts, disguised as a human, guiding Tobias along the way and instructing him on what to do.

❧ Angel Gabriel

You can ask God to send Angel Gabriel to help you:

- Connect with your feminine side.
- Receive a message from your spirit.
- Celebrate your life.
- Manifest your deepest desire.
- Cleanse your body, mind, home, and spirit.
- Be protected in violent weather or in travel.

Gabriel stands in the presence of God and is one of the two highest-ranking angels. He is a messenger whose symbol is the trumpet. Gabriel buried Moses. He announced the birth of John the Baptist to the world. Gabriel brings a message of hope to mankind. He reminds everyone of the importance of loving one another. He encourages unity and oneness. He brings mercy, forgiveness, change, and transformation.

Angel Gabriel Brings Messages

It is assumed that Gabriel is an archangel even though the scriptures do not give him the title of an archangel. He is a very powerful angel. The word archangel is defined as an angel of high rank. Gabriel's name deriving from the Hebrew language means, "Power of God" or "God is Mighty." He brings God's messages to humans, making the messages understandable to us. He helps us to listen with a heart of purity and to accept the will of God, the Almighty.

Gabriel is associated with the moon. He often makes his presence known with a flash of silver light. He also rules the element of water and is associated with the direction of the west. He helps with intuitive insights, herbal medicine, and women's menstrual cycles (Peck, On the Nine Ranks of Angels, 2014).

Gabriel also chooses which souls will be born. He spends nine months with the baby's spirit, helping the spirit adjust to the exciting journey of life on Earth. When the child is born, he causes the child to forget the secrets of heaven by pressing his finger below the baby's nose. Gabriel is a messenger archangel.

He gave important messages to God's people in the Bible (Peck, On the Nine Ranks of Angels, 2014). Gabriel can grant wishes, bring joy, unveil divine mysteries, reveal the truth, and grant justice. Gabriel can protect you from violent weather and make your travel easy and effortless. (Cited from, The Complete Encyclopedia of Angels, 2009, pg.22).

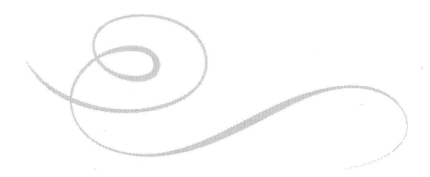

Hearing from the Spirit

"*Give God (Jehovah) His Glory. Worship Him, give Him praise often. Stay in the Word of God which means to meditate and study. Staying close to Him gives beauty in season and out of season. Spiritual beauty will you obtain; you will see that the closer you get to Him more spiritual beauty will be added; that is what He gives.*

"*When you worship God (Jehovah), pray and trust (Jehovah), He keeps you from obstacles that you cannot see or know. Keep a pattern of worshipping Him with song, dance, and music, later you will see how negative energies fall and your healing can begin. Do not take this lightly, the power of praising God. Singing to Him, adore Him, dance unto Him, you will see the positive effects of it when you consistently worship Him.*"

Holiness is Still Prioritized

"*Cleanse your temple which is the body He gave you. Cleansing your temple requires the practice of holiness. God says those that keep their temple clean with holiness will have His everlasting spring of life. God (Jehovah) wants us to live a cleansed life, free from things that pollute and defile the body. This process draws you closer to Him and allows your gifts to grow.*" *Even when we detour from our divine paths and make mistakes. God is always urging us to move back into a more positive way of life.*

"*Be mindful to confess your sins. No one is perfect here on this earth. Confession of* sin is important; it keeps us close to the Heavenly Father. We must be sorry for our sins. When we follow and draw close to God, we will experience more joy and peace in this life."

Confession is a part of cleansing, and this compares to spiritual breathing in and out.

"Being kind is important and some people do not understand how important this spiritual concept is. Kindness is the product of having the fruits of the Holy Spirit. It gives strength to you as a person and blesses the receiver. Set out today and as much as possible to be a blessing to those that you are inspired to show kindness to from your heart." **"But the fruit of the Spirit is love, joy, peace, longsuffering, gentleness, goodness, faith, meekness, temperance: against such there is no law."** (Galatians 5:22-23). Goodness refers to kindness, generosity, and benevolence. Be mindful that God hears the prayers of the righteous according to the scriptures. 1 Peter 3:12 **"For the eyes of the Lord are over the righteous, and his ears are open unto their prayers: but the face of the Lord is against them that do evil."**

"In the last days, there will be higher than normal angelic activity in the earth from the hand of God".

My Father's Angelic Experience

THERE WAS AN EMPLOYEE COOKOUT FOR MY STEPMOTHER'S COMPANY. DAD WAS excited about attending the gathering. He invited my children and me to the event. I drove over to Dad's house to meet them there with my children. I waited outside in my car for about thirty minutes. Suddenly, a large crowd of crows and ravens congregated on top of the roof of Dad's house.

There were many crows and ravens which almost covered the entire roof. Seeing that many birds was unusual to me and that is what intrigued me to pay attention. The birds began to make a cawing sound together. They were cawing very loudly as if they were trying to warn us of something.

Warnings of Danger Given

I knew in my spirit that God was using the crows and ravens to convey a message that we were about to experience something serious, which could be death around the corner. I stayed calm within myself during this experience. I was trying to think about where this experience of seriousness could come from. Where was the danger or death? I could not figure it out. I thought to myself about what was going on during the moment. What I decided to do was to repeat Psalm 23 out loud. After repeating the 23rd Psalm I forgot about the situation and did not think any more about it even though the crows and ravens were still on the roof.

Before we left their house for the short trip out of town, my dad made sure that everyone was buckled in. He said, "Everyone put on your seat belts." When we arrived, there was a big crowd of people playing board games, cards, dancing, barbecuing, and eating other good foods. It was a beautiful warm sunny day. The lake was glistening from the sun shining on it. Ducks were swimming across the lake. People were in canoes paddling across the lake. It was such a beautiful day.

Enjoying The Fun

People were on the lake riding in canoes having a good time with their families and coworkers. Everyone was having a good time. Later during the day, many gathered to the dance floor to do that old dance favorite, the electric slide. My dad was on the dance floor with my stepmom. Dad enjoyed group dancing and was a very good dancer. He had won awards for dancing.

Finally, the cookout and party came to a halt. Some of the people there began leaving the park. When I saw other people leaving in large groups; I wanted to leave too. I started asking Dad if he was ready to go. I continued to have an urgent strong feeling that we needed to leave right away for some reason. Dad was ready to go as well, however, he was constantly stalling when trying to get ready to go. He wanted to finish a card game. Finally, we started on our way out of the park too. We had not driven far down the road from the park when suddenly, a car was approaching us from the opposite direction head-on.

We were traveling north, and the other car was traveling south toward the park. Before my dad had a chance to react to the car which was coming full force towards us at the speed of all most 70mph down the residential street, we were both on. The car slammed with a heavy impact into the front of the van on my dad's side.

A Lingering Negative Impact

This dramatic impact was the beginning of an event that changed our lives for a long, long time. We were a little in shock; the accident happened fast. The first thing I remember doing was holding my son's car seat in place. My eyes were on him even though the car was about to overturn. I could see that the impact was very forceful. Even though my son was strapped in securely, the seat belt was not strong enough to keep him from being thrown out of the window.

Then I looked to my left and my daughter's head hit the window hard. It happened quickly and I was not able to stop it. While I was looking at her, my neck was jerked very hard to the right as if it was being broken. The impact had knocked all the bobby pins out of my hair. My stepmom's bottom lip had a deep split on it. Her knees somehow hit against something in the van which made her knees fill with swelling and fluid.

My dad cried out "I'm stuck, my ankle is stuck in the bent part of the van's door." The van's door had metal around my dad's ankle. Then we realized that the van was smoking and trying to catch fire. I was in a lot of pain. My stepmom, the children, and I got out of the van. My dad could not get out of the van. He was trapped inside. He knew that the situation was not one that we could help him with. Within about 15 to 20 minutes or more a fire truck came out of nowhere. They got the Jaws of Life tool out and rescued my dad.

Angels On the Scene

Dad never said that he saw Archangel Michael. However, he did say that he asked God to send Archangel Michael because he needed urgent assistance from a dangerous situation. He knew that his prayers to God had been answered. Dad was taken to the hospital in a coma. He was in a coma for three days. His ankle had to be rebuilt. There were rods and pins placed in him from broken bones. When I went to see my dad in the hospital, he told me what happened to him during the accident.

He said "I knew that no one could help that was around me. I decided to ask God to send Archangel Michael to help get me out of a dangerous situation. Then before I knew it, a fire truck appeared out of nowhere and got me out of the smoking van." He told us, that he knew to ask God for this intervention. Once he decided to call out to God for Archangel Michael's assistance, immediate help came for him. My dad never forgot this help from God. He was very grateful that God allowed one of his glorious ones, the Archangel Michael to help him. Not only did my dad get help from the angelic ones, the driver of the other car received immediate help as well.

After the uproar of the incident, my family and I had no way to get home. We were about 75 miles from our residence. Nighttime was soon around the corner. I had two small children in an isolated area that were exhausted and injured by the events of that day. As we were standing there outside in a strange town with no public transportation, my thoughts were about what to do next. I had no idea.

Nighttime had arrived and we were standing on the side of the road alone. Suddenly two cars came up and I realized that it was my dad's brother and niece. We were so grateful to see them pull up. We thought that we were forgotten. Shout out to Uncle Rufus and Candace. I could sing hallelujah to God every time the memory comes to me of the unexpected help we received. They were operating as God's earthly angels for us. Their kindness and thoughtfulness will always be appreciated.

Dad Praising God for His Goodness

My Dad never forgot God's goodness and lovingkindness that was given to him that day as well. He continued to remind us how God allowed Archangel Michael to hear his urgent petition for immediate help. He told others about this rescue and encouraged others to ask God for this kind of assistance. I'm glad that Dad had the encouragement and courage to share his experiences. Glory be to God for His protection.

Angels work through everyday people too, blessing mankind through their earthly jobs. I must personally thank God for His intervention and for how He managed to keep all of us in the van from experiencing worse. I do believe that repeating Psalm 23 before starting our journey to the lake, helped to keep us all from early death as well.

My dad reminded us that angels are divine helpers sent from God to humans. One of his favorite angels was Archangel Michael. Every time Dad visited our home he talked about Archangel Michael. He never informed us of seeing an angel. However, he did have divine encounters which he felt involved the miraculous help of Archangel Michael.

The after-effects of this accident changed our lives. My daughter was experiencing blackouts and had to be taken to a neurologist several times. I began to have blackouts when trying to drive a car. I had to stop driving and get others to take me around. My back was in constant pain for many years. My son had a difficult time walking for a while without limping. My Dad would always have rods and pins in his body. It was a deadly event that we encountered and could have shortened our lives instantly. It was such a dramatic experience that stayed in our memories for years. The effects of this dramatic experience caused many changes in our health and lifestyle.

Angelic Protection Given

I WAS HAVING TROUBLE WITH A VAN THAT ONE OF MY RELATIVES LET ME USE. THE BRAKES continued to be a problem after getting them serviced several times. The van was in my yard for a while without being driven. I decided to start using it with my relative's permission. I could clearly see that sometimes the van had a difficult time stopping with a little slide to it. Later that week I decided to take it to a different place to be serviced. The Goodyear Center was selected to get the brakes checked and repaired before driving it on a regular basis.

I got in the van with my daughter and went down my driveway. She was about 12 years old then. We stopped at the bottom of the driveway. I stood there for a few minutes to look out for ongoing traffic. We live on a busy main street. While I stood there my daughter said, "Mommy I see Archangel Michael standing across the street". I said to myself, how can she see that when I don't see anything? I asked her, "Where is the angel?" She said, "he is right there across the street, and don't you see him too"? She said, "he is standing right there looking toward us." I said nothing and forgot about the situation. I wanted to hurry and get to Goodyear Auto Services in the van we were traveling in.

Angels There When Needed

We finally reached Goodyear. I drove the van into the line to be checked. Once the van was diagnosed by the mechanic; he asked me how I got there to them. I told him that I drove the van. He said "I don't see how you got here driving the van. I asked him why he was saying that. He said, "I'm saying that because you have no brakes at all. How were you able to drive this van here?" He asked me if I was able to stop at intersections and red lights.

I told him that I had no problems stopping the van on my way to be serviced. I just looked at him with amazement. It took me a couple of days to realize that we were under angelic protection, His glorious angels. Even though I never saw Archangel Michael, I knew that my daughter did see an angel. I'm not sure if it was Michael or not. Maybe that was the only name she knew to call the angel at the time. She was very accustomed to my dad talking about Archangel Michael all the time.

Angelic Impression Experience

I wasn't sure why I wanted to ask God for angelic help. It was placed in my thoughts to ask God for it. The specific angel that I asked God to send for assistance was Archangel Uriel. The feeling would not go away for a few minutes that I needed to ask God for help. I strongly felt that even though nothing seemed to be apparently significant in making the request, nevertheless it should be done. There was a strong impression on my mind to do it. After making this prayer request, I was in my bedroom when intriguing thoughts started to come through. The thoughts were that I should go downstairs and check to make sure that all the windows were locked and secure.

During that time, I had never had any thoughts to check my windows since living in my home for almost twenty years. My thoughts led me downstairs to check on the windows again and again. If I had not been quiet enough to hear my thoughts, which were answers to my prayers, the outcome could have been a negative one. To my surprise, every lock on each window had been deliberately broken off. It really shook me for a minute to see all twelve windows with broken locks. It was obvious that someone was planning to come in. Before this incident, we had several people staying in the house. My next decision was to thank God for allowing His angel to assist me with the information. I will never know if God sent Uriel specifically or not. However, I do know that an angel did intervene. I had no way of knowing what was revealed to me on my own.

Afterward, I was able to quickly get someone to take off the broken locks and replace them with new locks. It gave me a feeling of relaxation to know that the new locks were installed. God is a good God! God sends angels to give us thoughts about what to do sometimes.

Angelic Experience and Animals

I have mentioned earlier in this book, that I have experienced several angelic experiences. I will share only certain ones in this book. Here is another one that I will talk about. When I was in my mid-thirties, life was getting a little more complex. More challenges with two people in the neighborhood had begun without my realization. Every day, I went to work to teach the handicapped children and come home to my family. I stayed busy in my immediate surroundings and had little time for socializing.

My main hobbies and enjoyment became relaxation, watching movies in bed, and developing lesson plans for my students. I enjoyed creating and obtaining tactile activities for my students to enjoy. Whenever I did go out to socialize with people, it was usually with co-workers. I would have a good time hanging out with them at restaurants and parties in the community that only teachers mostly attended. Going to restaurants that I had never been to in my own state was enjoyable with the other teachers. I was usually the quiet one in the group. I had nothing to say which they probably thought was mysterious. They probably had no idea how much I enjoyed going to different events with them when there was an opportunity. It was my little secret.

A relationship with distant kin I had in the past, close to my house, began to get sour without my knowledge about it. I had not seen this person in a couple of years, and they had not come to mind in a while. Little did I know that there was a problem brewing between the two of us. There was no indication of a problem on my side. In the background, trouble had come my way for what reason, I had no idea.

The strange part about it was, there was no indication of this person's hostility towards me until angelic intervention came my way! I did hear about this person's bad intentions toward me from an unlikely source. I felt that I needed to ask God for protection anyway. I had heard talk of this person wanting to cause a problem for me.

Most likely the person wanted to do me physical harm. However, I could not understand where the hostility was coming from towards me. The person never tried to communicate with me or visit me to reconcile any disagreements or conflicts. I had no idea how to mend any disputes when I did not know how to reach the person.

Angelic Help Was There

A friend of the person that wanted to harm me in some way told me many months later what happened. The friend lived with the person for a couple of years in the neighborhood. They were not far away from my home. They did many things together and knew each other for many years. For many years, they worked on the same projects at the same job.

One day, when I was at home, the friend came to me and said, "Sheryl you will not believe what happened." I was given all the details of what took place. To make a long story short, I was told that the person had headed out of the door to start a fight with me. Then suddenly, as they approached the doorway to go outside, an animal attacked the individual. The animal did not cause any real harm. It was a surprise of divine timing. I thanked God for sending His angels to intervene! God does use animals to act for Him sometimes.

Angels Stopping the Car

A church member that I knew enjoyed talking about God and His goodness to her. She was a very spiritual person that loved God. She liked talking about how good her 20-year marriage was. She went into specific details in explaining the deep spiritual connection that was within her marriage. I was very interested in her conversation. It was amazing to hear how spiritually connected they were. It was hard to believe that two people could be that connected. I was wondering in my mind how in the world could I obtain a spiritual connection with my husband like that. It made me feel joyful inside to know that a strong spiritual connection could exist between a husband and wife.

I was having a good day with her and listened carefully to the conversation. However, in the back of my mind, I was thinking about some serious car maintenance that I needed on my Corvette. These thoughts about the car were a clear distraction and I did not take to heart anything that she was saying about marriage. Driving that car to work and back was such a delight. Hearing the engine of the Corvette roar like a lion was very pleasurable and exciting. My regular routine was to get up at around 5:30 am in the morning to get started for work, to teach school and to get my daughter ready for daycare.

Since I could not get the car issues off my mind while conversating with her; I asked her for a recommendation to a good company that specializes in car brakes. She told me the name of the company and its location. The next day, I drove my car to the company with no issues. They called me at the end of the day to pick up the car. I drove it home. Everything appeared to be working appropriately with the brakes. I had no trouble stopping it for red lights and stopping signs.

A new day had begun, and I was doing my normal routines of getting ready for work to teach and to get my daughter ready. As I was getting my daughter ready for daycare, she did not appear to be feeling well. I called a family member to take care of her for me. My daughter needed to stay with the relative until I got home from work. Those were my plans for my daughter for that day.

Finally, it was time for me to get off work. Within my thoughts, I knew that my daughter probably still was not feeling well. Therefore, I wanted to hurry to pick her up. I got into the Corvette and buckled the seat belt. Then I proceeded to drive and get on the highway, in my mind I had to hurry. The driving distance from my job to where my daughter was located was about twenty-five miles.

I got on the highway and began to increase the speed until I was at about 85 mph. The speed limit at that time was 65 mph. Anyway, I was speeding and increasing speed to hurry. The exit that I needed was about a mile and half down the highway. The thought came to me that I needed to start slowing down, even though the exit was about a mile and a half away. I don't even know why this thought came to mind repeatedly.

Angelic Help Not Far Away

I followed the small voice inside and tried to slow down. I took my foot off the accelerator and then tried to use the brakes some. That is when I realized that I had no brakes. The car would not slow down, and I had no brakes to stop or slow the car down with. For some odd reason. I did not panic. I was trying to think of what to do next. A thought came to me quickly. I was thinking the only thing I could do at that point was to try to exit and turn the car into the embankment off the exit to stop.

To my surprise after getting closer to the exit about half a mile away, the car began to slow down on its own. The car went from 85 mph to 65mph to 35 mph and on down to 5 mph. After slowing completely down I was now at the exit stop sign. I was able to exit off the highway safely. After exiting, the car stopped on its own with no brakes. I did not even have my feet on the brakes to try to stop because there were no brakes. Then I was able to put the car in the park and pull up the emergency brakes.

I had to tell the relative that I would have to get another way to pick my daughter up. They were patient with me because I told them what happened. Before even thinking about picking her up, I had a tow truck to take the car back to where I had it serviced. When I got there in the tow truck, they waited on me right away. When checking out the car again they told me that the brakes were not put on correctly. I was not angry at them. I just knew that I would never go there again nor recommend them to anyone.

God's angels were there for me during the midst of a bad storm. I was so thankful to God! I did not have time to be angry with those people. I asked them, why would they have mechanics working on brakes when they are new to the trade with no experience. The church member may have led me to the wrong place; however, the entire experience became a miracle for me that I will never ever forget.

While reflecting on the conversations with the church member, I realized that she was sent to me for a specific purpose. I was supposed to listen to how she strengthened her marriage. If I was really paying attention as needed and more sensitive to spiritual visitations, it would have been easier for me to recognize. That was her purpose that day to talk about marriage; how to develop not only a physical closeness but a spiritual closeness in marriage as well. Therefore, I can say that I missed the entire point of her visit.

Breaking the Step

One night I decided to turn my cable on to watch television. The program selected was a religious program and they were talking about angels and God's protection. The subject interested me because they were giving real-life examples of how angels had protected others. I felt that God was talking to me through this program. I listened and thought about God's protection given through angelic intervention to help everyday people. Later, during the same month, I turned on the television again and spotted another religious program discussing angels.

In my mind, it seemed evident to me that God was really trying to get my attention for some reason. Never had I viewed religious television programming emphasizing angels this often. I wondered why I continued to see programming like this. Weeks later, I began to realize that God was trying to let me know that He will provide angelic help to me when I needed it.

Angelic Activity Foretelling in Dreams

One day, my son came to me and told me that he had a dream about someone dying from a gruesome head injury that was caused by a bear. The dream was hard to understand, and why he would be having such a dream was difficult for me to figure out. He did not know who the person was in the dream and how the seriously injured person would come into contact with a bear.

The dream also had a lot of details which made it even more confusing. It was a very long dream. The main events that stood out to me were the severely injured head injury and the bear. I told my son that I did not understand the dream; however, it appeared to be trying to help us by revealing an urgent future event. We both tried to figure out the details to no avail. What was this dream trying to tell my son and me? Why did he dream about a bear when we do not have bears in our town?

During the month of November in 2006, I never thought that we would experience the dream that my son had. That night in November was a dark and cold one. I was on my daughter's laptop at home trying to shop with a list of items given to me for a wheelchair-bound woman. Here I am thinking everything was all right and normal. I went into the den and told the children to turn the television down, the volume was too high. Then I went to the back of the house to complete the shopping. The television was never turned down.

Angelic Messages Unfolding

Around 8:30 pm that same night, a frightening event took place at our home. There was a home invasion inside of our home. That night the house has up and downstairs. That night the television was up very loud and suddenly, my daughter said yelling, "Mom I hear banging, loud banging, and it sounds like someone knocked the door down in the downstairs area."

There were six family members upstairs and three people downstairs. I did not hear the banging noise, but my daughter became more nervous and asked me to listen next to the locked hall door. When I heard the noise, I called 911. We did not know what to do. My mother began to walk around in circles and was acting very confused. I gave the dispatcher all the information and she told me to stay on the phone. I was on the phone for about 10 minutes when suddenly the intruder began to walk up the steps to come upstairs. My heart began to pound, and I had no idea what to do.

The intruder had a lot of keys that made a lot of noise. For that reason, we could hear very well that the person was starting to come upstairs to where we were. I began to get nervous. Then suddenly, we heard another very loud noise that came from downstairs. Then suddenly the intruder stopped walking upstairs. There was complete silence. Meanwhile, we waited for the police to arrive at the house and check everything out. The polices told us that the back door had been kicked in and someone had been killed with a severely injured head injury.

They looked around for hours in the dark with flashlights to find the weapon used. They told us that it had to be a blunt object. The police could not find the object anywhere. This was a frightening experience for everyone involved. After this entire ordeal, weeks afterward I was finally able to go down the stairs.

Immediately I noticed that one step on the staircase was broken into pieces. I knew that God protected us with His angels. The broken step stopped the intruder from going further up the steps toward us. Now, I understood why I continued to see television programming about angels and why my son remembered to tell me his dream. He was only about seven years old at that time. I never expected that we would experience that kind of danger. It was an awfully hard experience to go through and we were grief-stricken about the deceased for a while.

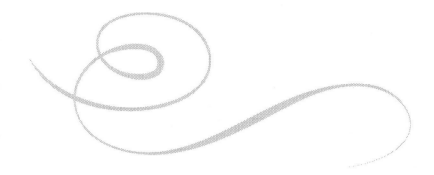

Meaning of Angelic Visitations

W HAT DOES IT MEAN TO HUMANS WHEN WE HAVE AN ANGELIC VISITATION? Angels appearing to us clarifies clearly that God is watching and supporting us, and that they have an important message to provide. Isn't it beautiful and comforting how God sends these angels to assist us? Each of us faces our own challenges, trials, and situations and it is comforting to know that God cares about these factors in our lives today. The support and appearances of angels are not just for the Biblical times, angels are here for us today.

There are angels to assist and help us in matters of love. Abraham in the Bible knew that God cared about every facet of his life and in the life of his family. He trusted God to send an angel to help his servant find the correct wife and helpmate for his son. The angel that Abraham depended on for this miracle did not appear physically. However, the miracle of love happened to his son. God can assist us with these matters of love today. God wants us to know that He is willing to help us find the appropriate partner in life. We don't have to worry and be confused about where, how, and when about finding an appropriate marriage partner. If it is God's will for an individual to be married, God delights in bringing the correct wife or husband.

An Aha Moment Appears Out of Thin Air!

Some visitations from Angels are available from God to help us obtain an understanding of difficult situations and issues in a greater way. Have you ever heard a person say, that they had an "aha moment" or as if a light bulb went off in their thoughts? What is an "aha moment" or moment of clarity? These are moments of thoughts and understanding that suddenly come upon you. During these moments you just know will provide a positive outcome or an answer of understanding to something that was puzzling or difficult to understand. They are like sudden moments of realization that was never thought of or overlooked.

People experiencing "aha moments" or moments of clarity have thoughts and ideas that appear to come out of nowhere on how to resolve an issue. These moments of thought are how angels communicate with humans sometimes to give them solutions to problems and provide miracle intervention. Remember Angels don't have to be physically present to provide miracles and intervention. Therefore, we do not need to seek physical appearances from Angels all the time. They only appear when God wants them to appear. He is in full control of how His Angels operate on the earth and in our lives.

When you experience those "aha moments" don't forget that you may be having an angelic experience and visitation. Those thoughts most likely are not your own. It appears that these "aha moments" can coincide with an individual's intuition process as well. How many times has your intuition kept you from danger, and difficult situations? Angels can and do send you feelings of intuition in times of danger or trouble. Intuition is the ability to know and to understand something without conscious reasoning or any external validation. Intuition gives the ability to tap into direct guidance which is the knowing of your soul and subconscious.

Your intuition and Angelic Intervention

If we pay attention closely, intuition will keep us from harmful people and situations. It will guide us toward the achievement of our goals. It can aid people in becoming more healthy, happy, abundant, and prosperous. In times of difficulties or potentially troublesome issues, an intuitive feeling or discerning spirit can come over you. This feeling of knowing is beyond logical reasoning and may come as an uneasy feeling within your stomach or as a feeling to take specific actions.

Some people experience hearing, seeing, or feeling intuitive impressions. And others have dreams. When intuitive impressions happen, you will know it. Try not to ignore it. Those impressions are your guardian angels and angelic visitations that will protect and guide you. These angelic visitations may even save your life. The question is, can intuition be your guardian angel? In many instances, it appears that intuition can be the voice of your guardian angel.

Intuition in Operation

For example, I had an urgent feeling that I should pray to God for my daughter. The thoughts came when I was not expecting them. I'm glad that I followed the feelings to pray. My daughter was in a very dangerous situation. She was driving one night to work in her van. Little did she know that the van caught on fire toward the passenger rear.

She stopped at a red light and intended to turn into the gas station to get gas. When she stopped for the light, a driver from behind her told her that fire was coming from the back. She was able to park the van in a safe location and get out of it. The van caught fire and burnt to the point it was unrepairable. She could do nothing about the fire but watch it burn.

Intuition Working to Protect

Another example of listening to our intuition serving as an angelic guide is taken from a blog on LinkedIn by Sista Joy (D. M. Foster). Here is her story in her own words and how she was protected using her intuition. *"It was the summer of 1973 and I had gone to see my brother. He was not home. As I started to leave, his wife and daughters called out for me to join them on their back porch. Their mean dog was there. As they beckoned, a terrible feeling came over me and I heard the warning, "danger." I ignored it and listened to them instead. "Oh, don't worry the dog is on a thick chain," they said. I believed them,* but the bad feeling persisted so powerfully, and a voice somewhere inside me urged me to at least take out my Pepper Spray, turn it on, and hold it in my hand. Thank God I did!

"Opening the gate, I walked through and started up the stairs. Their dog just sat there watching, until I put my foot down on the top step. Then he lunged at me, snapping and snarling. Terrified, I ran down the stairs and back through the yard trying to get to the gate. Before I could, he broke his chain, leaped over the porch banister, and came after me full force. It happened so quickly that everyone just stood there shocked and screaming.

A big, strong German Shepherd that was trained to attack, grabbed the back of my pants, jerked my legs out from under me, and down I went, falling on my back. When I looked up, it was into the cold-blooded eyes of this vicious beast. I knew, instinctively, his intent was to tear my face off or throat out!

Only seconds away from coming down to do it, I blasted him with my Pepper Spray. Aiming for his eyes, I pumped it with all my might. Once, twice, three times - whew! Thank God, it worked. It stopped him in his tracks. As he moved away pawing his eyes, I jumped up and ran for my life. It shook me to my very core" (Foster, 2015).

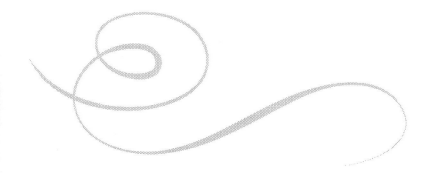

Golden Deeds

W E CANNOT UNDERESTIMATE THE POWER OF HELPING THOSE LESS FORTUNATE or going through hard times. This is a very important spiritual concept as well. The Bible has many references to helping the poor and the benefits of doing that. Helping the poor is admonished throughout the Bible. You may wonder how does helping the poor activate angelic activity.

Assisting the poor may not appear to have connections with obtaining angelic help. However, giving alms does contribute to the help that the angelic realm provides. There are several examples in the Bible that show us how certain people had lives full of charitable deeds, not just good deeds that are done every now and then. It was a way of life for them.

Activating Angels Through Our Deeds

There are many verses in the Holy Bible written regarding helping and considering those that are limited in financial resources. For example, Psalm 41:1-3 states that those who consider the poor have certain benefits and the Lord delivers them on the day of trouble. The scriptures read the following, *blessed is he that considereth the poor: the Lord will deliver him in time of trouble. The Lord will preserve him, and keep him alive, and he shall be blessed upon the earth: and thou wilt not deliver him unto the will of his enemies.*

The Lord will strengthen him upon the bed of languishing: thou will make all his bed in his sickness Psalm 41:1-3. We cannot ignore those that are in need.

Caesarea is known as Cornelius the Centurion of a band called the Italian band. The entire chapter of Acts 10 gives the details of how prayer and alms aided him in obtaining a vision of an angel of God. This vision that Cornelius saw was about the ninth hour of the day. He was a devout man that feared God.

During this vision of Cornelius, which was accompanied by prayer and fasting, the angel of the Lord said that his prayers and alms had come up before God as a memorial. The angel of the Lord gave Cornelius specific instructions of whom to send where and when, how, why, and who should be called on for assistance. These divine instructions led Cornelius to take specific actions.

Helping Others Brings Spiritual Assistant

Job was father to the needy in Job 29:16. He grieved for the needy. Job also made the hearts of widows sing. He was full of good deeds toward others in need. The Bible speaks of Job being a man that fears God and stays away from evil. Job did many good deeds and alms for people. God in return blessed him with prosperity. The scriptures say that God had a hedge of protection around Job and his family (Job 1:10).

One of the characteristics of the virtuous woman in Proverbs 31:20 is that she helps the poor and needy. Dorcas was abounding in good deeds of kindness and charity, which she did not do sometimes but continually. She did not stop showing kindness (Acts 9:36). Dorcas was protected from death and raised up from severe sickness.

Prayers for Protection

WHY IS PRAYER IMPORTANT? PRAYER HELPS US TO OPEN OUR HEARTS TO GOD. Through prayers, He will transform our lives and provide answers and miracles. I have witnessed myself the power of praying Psalm 23. A friend of my mother's was skeptical about his safety. We were walking together in a plaza parking lot. He began repeating 23rd Psalm out loud several times around me. I had no idea that he did not feel safe within the current environment. When he began repeating the 23rd Psalm, I did take special notice of him. Months, later I realized he omitted dangerous events all around him. This memory, I can not forget.

PRAYER of Confession

Heavenly Father, thank you for your mercy, truth, and compassion in my life. Each moment in your presence, Lord is a delight. Thank you for all your blessings. I confess my sins and wrongdoings now before you. You said in your Word in I John 1:9 that if we confess our sins, you are faithful and just to forgive. I'm now pausing in this moment of prayer to self-reflect on those incorrect actions and ask you to forgive me. Fill me with your Holy Spirit that I may partake of your kingdom and be given your love, joy, peace, goodness, and faith. Help me not to walk in a spirit of anger or bitterness against those that have offended me. Help me to be a more fulfilled person. Show me how to be led by Your Spirit. In the mighty name of Jesus Christ, Amen.

PRAYER of Angelic Protection

Heavenly Father, provide your angelic protection for me throughout the day. Send Archangel Michael to be with me and around me. You said in Your Holy Word, Psalm 91, that your angels will protect me, thank you. Thank you for allowing your angels to watch over me, to guide me into the right paths and correct actions. Cover me and surround me with an angelic presence. Let the words of my mouth be acceptable to you today. Help me the Holy Spirit to speak life, which are the right words over my situations and over other people. Oh, Lord guard my mouth to speak according to Your Word. Give me a strong desire in my heart to be a light unto others and to serve You in ways that are pleasing to You. In Jesus Christ's name, Amen.

Prayer of Guidance and Protection

The Lord is my shepherd; I shall not want. He makes me lie down in green pastures. He leads me beside still waters. He restores my soul. He leads me in paths of righteousness for his name's sake. Even though I walk through the valley of the shadow of death, I will fear no evil, for you are with me; your rod and your staff, they comfort me. You prepare a table before me in the presence of my enemies; you anoint my head with oil; my cup overflows (Psalm 23).

PRAYER of Pleading the Blood

Heavenly Father, I ask you in the name of your son Jesus Christ for protection by the blood of Jesus over my house and family. I am pleading with the blood of Jesus that washes away my sins to protect my vehicle when traveling and all my activities today. I pray for a covering of protection through the blood of Jesus over my spirit and mind from witchcraft, black magic, sorcery, the evil eye, or evil intents against me or my family.

Cover me with the precious blood of your son Jesus Christ and each member of my family. I'm pleading the blood of Jesus to protect me, my family, friends, and acquaintances from all diseases, accidents, misfortunes, and sudden deaths. Let the blood of Jesus Christ protect my job, my business activities, financial decisions, and transactions In Jesus's Christ name, I pray Amen.

The Lord's Prayer

Our Father, who art in heaven,
hallowed be thy Name,
thy kingdom come,
thy will be done,
on earth as it is in heaven.

Give us this day our daily bread.
And forgive us our trespasses,
as we forgive those
who trespass against us.

And lead us not into temptation,
but deliver us from evil.

For thine is the kingdom,
and the power, and the glory,
forever and ever. Amen.

Psalm 91

He that dwelleth in the secret place of the most High shall abide under the shadow of the Almighty. I will say of the Lord, He is my refuge and my fortress: my God; in him will I trust. Surely, he shall deliver thee from the snare of the fowler, and from the noisome pestilence. He shall cover thee with his feathers, and under his wings shalt thou trust: his truth shall be thy shield and buckler. Thou shalt not be afraid for the terror by night; nor for the arrow that flieth by day; Nor for the pestilence that walketh in darkness; nor for the destruction that wasteth at noonday. A thousand shall fall at thy side, and ten thousand at thy right hand; but it shall not come nigh thee. Only with thine eyes shalt thou behold and see the reward of the wicked.

Because thou hast made the Lord, which is my refuge, even the Most High, thy habitation; There shall no evil befall thee, neither shall any plague come nigh thy dwelling. For he shall give his angels charge over thee, to keep thee in all thy ways. They shall bear thee up in their hands, lest thou dash thy foot against a stone. Thou shalt tread upon the lion and adder: the young lion and the dragon shalt thou trample under feet. Because he hath set his love upon me, therefore will I deliver him: I will set him on high, because he hath known my name. He shall call upon me, and I will answer him: I will be with him in trouble; I will deliver him and honour him. With long life will I satisfy him and shew him my salvation.

Prayer for School

Heavenly Father, please protect me while I'm at school and place your angels around me while there. Keep away those individuals that want to bully me or turn me away from following your perfect will for my life. Your holy words say in Jeremiah 29:11 that you have plans to prosper me and to give me hope. Surround me with loving and supportive friends at school. Help me to be a good friend to those that you bring my way to embrace. Show me how to organize my school day and build my confidence to learn new material. Give me the discipline that I need to be a good student. Open my mind to embrace new concepts for learning with ease. Help me to comprehend and remember what I learn in school in Jesus Christ's Name, Amen.

Jesus Christ Carried the Penalties of Our Sins

THESE GLORIOUS ANGELS OF GOD ARE READY TO ASSIST US WITH LIFE TRIALS, tribulations, and to help bring the miracles that are needed. We can ask in prayer to God for angelic help through His Son, Jesus Christ. It is a good idea to have a relationship with God. Call out to Him to save your soul through His Son Jesus the Messiah. We are sinners and need a Savior. I do not have a background without any faults. We can carry all our sins, mistakes, and errors to the cross. Some people may never forget our past sins, errors, and mistakes. The enemy can use situations like that to try and hold us captive to our past mistakes and sins.

Jesus Christ came to redeem mankind from sin. He came to give us an abundant life, to live past our regrets and mistakes. God said in His Word that when we confess and forsake our sins; He tosses them into the sea of forgetfulness. The scriptures state in *Micah 7:19 He will turn again; he will have compassion upon us; he will subdue our iniquities, and thou wilt cast all their sins into the depths of the sea.* Who then can be forgiven by Jehovah (God)? Those individuals that confess and forsake past offenses and their goal is to be the best version of themselves, which is to be more like Jesus Christ.

The Reality of Spiritual Warfare

I have noticed in my own life that the closer I get to Jesus Christ, spiritual warfare starts. Some people that I don't even know will start to bring up negative things that I did as a child under 12. When trying to draw closer to Jesus Christ, and the works of Christ there can come the opposition out of nowhere. Spiritual warfare is very real, and it is there not for correction. I experienced spiritual attacks while writing this book writing this book for some reason.

Sometimes, it is not easy to believe that help is readily available. We need to be sure that we come to God's throne confessing our sins, with a heart of intentions to give true repentance and pure intentions. God favors righteousness, and righteousness is two-fold.

The first part of righteousness is that Jesus Christ gives us righteousness with God.

The second part of righteousness involves right action, right thinking, and faith. These attributes help us to be more available to Divine assistance. Holy men in the Bible, who were inspired by God's Holy Spirit, revealed that the prayers of the righteous avails much. The effectual fervent prayer of a righteous man availeth much, according to James 5:16.

What does "effectual fervent prayer" really imply? Effectual really means producing a desired result or effect and the definition for fervent is to exhibit or be marked by great intensity of feeling. In other words, the "effectual fervent prayers" are prayers that we speak in faith, knowing that the desired result is already manifest in the Kingdom of God and on Earth. When we call on the name of Jesus Christ in faith, angels are put on assignments to aid us.

Author's Notes

ANGELS HELP US IN MANY WAYS IN LIFE, EVEN IN SOME WAYS THAT MAY GO unrecognized. God is a loving God and shows humanity His love and kindness. He has countless angels that act on His command and Word. We are admonished in the word of God to be kind to strangers. It is important that we do not forget to show hospitality to strangers. "Be not forgetful to entertain strangers: for thereby some have entertained angels unawares" (Hebrews 13: 2).

Going through this written journey reminds me of how loving and good God has been in past experiences to my family and me. I believe God continues to work on behalf of humanity, and through humanity, allowing us to come in contact with helpful and supportive individuals as well. Individuals that operate as earth angels are very helpful. These individuals allowed God to use them to promote divine assistance to people and society. I'm glad that my father spent time talking to my daughter and me about angels. This gave us the chance to know the spiritual world beyond what cannot be readily seen. This spiritual world is far more real than the world as we know it to be. This unseen realm is the realm of the Spirit of the Most High God and other spiritual beings.

I never fully understood at the time why my dad talked often about angels. During each visitation, my dad's main conversation was about the subject of angels. He always discussed the topic of angels. Now twenty years or more later, I understand better the reasons why. I'm glad that God used my dad as His mouthpiece. Little did I know that angelic activity was greatly active in the works of God and the world. God wanted us to know that help was available to us through His glorious angels.

The reasons that I have been led to write more in-depth about the many aspects and roles of God's angels are several. First, I'm hoping that by reading this book faith will increase inside of the heart and mind of the reader. Secondly, my goal was to build knowledge that maybe the reader did not have before and learn more facts about angels that they did not know. Thirdly, to increase awareness of angelic activity within practical everyday activities when we pray using the name of Jesus Christ our redeemer. Pressing forward and releasing faith to God opens a whole new positive realm of life.

Book Review

1. What do you understand about Angels?

2. Write down why Angels assisted certain people in the Bible.

3. Why do you think kindness is important to God?

4. What will you do to increase acts of kindness?

5. The witness of individual experiences lets us know that angelic activity and intervention is still active today. How are divine instructions given to people in biblical days?

6. What are Archangels?

Bibliographies

Sources

https://www.christianity.com/wiki/angels-and-demons/who-are-the-seraphim-in-the-bible.html

https://www.beliefnet.com/inspiration/angels/what-are-the-9-orders-of-angels.aspx

https://biblehub.com/hebrews/12-22.htm

https://www.desiringgod.org/articles/the-surprising-role-of-guardian-angels

https://biblehub.com/topical/s/sons_of_god.htm

https://www.holyart.com/blog/saints-and-blessed/archangels-who-are-they-and-what-is-their-function/

https://www.biblegateway.com/passage/?search=Matthew+18%3A10&version=KJV

https://bible.org/article/angelology-doctrine-angels

https://preachersinstitute.com/2014/12/05/on-the-nine-ranks-of-angels/

http://www2.iath.virginia.edu/anderson/vita/tables/vita.table7.html

https://www.linkedin.com/pulse/intuition-could-your-guardian-angel-d-m-sista-joy-foster/

https://www.guideposts.org/better-living/travel/7-of-the-worlds-amazing-healing-waters

Hopler, Whitney (2021, February 8). Archangel Gabriel's Messages in Dreams. Retrieved from https://www.learnreligions.com/archangel-gabriels-messages-in-dreams-123926

Britannica, T. Editors of Encyclopedia (Invalid Date). Cherub. Encyclopedia Britannica. https://www.britannica.com/topic/cherub

https://preachersinstitute.com/2014/12/05/on-the-nine-ranks-of-angels/ Home / Sermon Resources / On The Nine Ranks of Angels. December 5, 2014 By Fr. John A. Peck

Hopler, Whitney (2020, August 27). Thrones Angels in the Christian Angel Hierarchy. Retrieved from https://www.learnreligions.com/what-are-thrones-angels-123921

Matthew Henry Bible Commentary, Ezekiel 10. https://www.christianity.com/bible/commentary.php?com=mh&b=26&c=10

New International Encyclopedia of Bible Characters. (2001). Zondervan.

Peck, On the Nine Ranks of Angels (2014).

Ptolemy Tompkins and Tyler Beddoes, Proof of Angels (2016).

The Complete Encyclopedia of Angels, 2009, pg.22.

Scripture References

Numbers 22:31	Isaiah 48:11	Matthews 1:20
Job 1:6	I Corinthians 10:31	Luke 1:19
Psalm 89:6	James 3:6	Genesis 18:1,2
Job 38:4-7	Proverbs 18:21	Genesis 18:4
Isaiah 14: 13-14	Psalm 34:7	Genesis 18:22
Hebrews 1:7	Nehemiah 9:6	Genesis 19:1
2 Kings 6:17	Luke 1: 28-31	Hebrew 12:22
Numbers 22:21-27	Nehemiah 9:6	Judges 13:3
Numbers 22:31-33	Luke 1:26	Judges 13:5
Psalm 103:20	Colossians 1:16	2 Kings 1:2-3
Hebrews 1:6	Job 1:8	2 Kings 1: 15
Isaiah 42:8	Genesis 37	2 Kings 1: 12
Acts 12:21-23	Acts 27:23,24	Genesis 16:7-9

Genesis 16: 10-12	Revelations 22:8,9	Matthews 4:8-11
Luke 2:9-14	Hebrews 1:7	Revelations 8:4
Daniel 6:11	Revelations 20:1-3	Hebrews 12:22
Psalm 34:7	Revelations 12: 7-11	Isaiah 6:12
Psalm 91:11	Revelations 12:10	Luke 1: 28-31
Genesis 28:16	Colossians 2:14-15	Acts 27:23-25
Genesis 28:16-18	I John 1:9	Acts 1: 10,11
Matthews 2:13	Hebrews 1:13-14	Galatians 5:22,23
Genesis 31:10-12	John 5: 1-9	Hebrews 13:2
Genesis 37:5-10	Hebrews 1:1-6,8	Micah 7:19
Genesis 4:6,7	Hebrews 1:4-14	James 5:16
Revelations 15:6	Isaiah 6:2-7	
Revelations 1:1	Isaiah 6:8	
Revelations 16	Ezekiel 10:20-22	
Revelations 16:1	Ezekiel 10:1-22	
Genesis 19: 1-16	Genesis 3:24	
Revelation 19:17*	Exodus 5:18	
2 Samuel 24: 15-16	Revelations 4:6	
II Kings 19:35	Colossians 1:16	
I Corinthians 10:10	Daniel 7:9	
Revelations 19:10	Matthews 4:1-4	

About the Author

Mrs. Sheryl Ann Glass has been a member of Popular Springs Methodist Church in Atlanta, GA for several years. Mrs. Glass was led to attend Carver Bible College from 2015-2017, which has been presently renamed Carver College in Atlanta, GA. She has three lovely adult children and six grandchildren in Atlanta, GA.

Sheryl has a background in the healthcare business. She majored in drama/speech at Georgia State University. She has obtained a M.A. in Human Behavior, a M.S. in IT specializing in software engineering from Capella University in Minneapolis, MN and a M.A. in Learning Disabilities from Clark-Atlanta University in Atlanta, GA. Her B.A. in drama was obtained at Georgia State University in Atlanta, GA in 1982.

Printed in the United States
by Baker & Taylor Publisher Services